A Treatise on the Soul and its Origin

A Treatise on the Soul and its Origin

St. Augustine

A Treatise on the Soul and its Origin

© Lighthouse Publishing 2018

Written by: St. Augustine (Nov.13 354 – Aug.28 430)
Translated by Peter Holmes and Robert Ernest Wallis
Revised by: Professor Benjamin B. Warfield, D.D
Updated into Modern U.S English by A.M. Overett (b. 1960)

All rights reserved. Without limiting the rights under copyright reserved above, no part of this publication may be reproduced, stored in a retrieval system, or transmitted, in any form or by any means (electronic, mechanical, photocopying, recording or otherwise), without the prior written permission of the copyright owner of this book.

Published by
Lighthouse Christian Publishing
SAN 257-4330
5531 Dufferin Drive
Savage, Minnesota, 55378
United States of America

www.lighthousechristianpublishing.com

EXTRACT FROM AUGUSTIN'S "RETRACTATIONS,"

Book II. Chap. 56,

ON THE FOLLOWING TREATISE, "DE ANIMA ET EJUS ORIGINE."

"At that time one Vincentius discovered in the possession of a certain presbyter called Peter, in Mauritania Cæsariensis, a little work of mine, in a particular passage of which, touching the origin of souls in individual men, I had confessed that I knew not whether they are propagated from the primeval soul of the first man, and from that by parental descent, or whether they are severally assigned to each person without propagation, as the first was to Adam; but that I was, at the same time, quite sure that the soul was not body, but spirit. In opposition to these opinions of mine, he addressed to this Peter two books, which were sent to me from Cæsarea by the monk Renatus. Having read these books, I replied in four others, —one addressed to the monk Renatus, another to the presbyter Peter, and two more to Victor himself. That to Peter, however, though it has all the lengthiness of a book, is yet only a letter, which I did not like to be kept separate from the other three works. In all of them, while discussing many points which were unavoidable, I defended my hesitancy on the point of the origin of the souls which are given to individual men; and I pointed out this man's many errors and presumptuous pravity. At the same time, I treated the young man as gently as I could, —not as one who ought to be denounced all out of hand, but as one who ought to be still instructed; and I accepted the account of his conduct which he wrote back to me. In this work of mine, the book addressed to Renatus begins with these words: "Your sincerity towards us;" while that which was written to Peter begins thus: "To his Lordship, my dearly beloved brother and co-presbyter Peter." Of the last two books, which are addressed to Vincentius Victor, the former one thus opens: "As to that which I have thought it my duty to write to you."

ADVERTISEMENT TO THE READER ON THE FOLLOWING TREATISE.

The occasion of these four books was furnished by a young man named Vincentius Victor, a native of Mauritania Cæsariensis, a convert to the catholic Church from the Rogatian faction (which split off from the Donatist schism, and inhabited that part of Mauritania which lay around Cartenna). This Victor, they say, had previously so high an opinion of the Vincentius who succeeded Rogatus as the head of the before-mentioned faction, that he adopted his name as his own. Happening to meet with a certain work of Augustin's, in which the writer acknowledged himself to be incapable of saying whether all souls were propagated from Adam's soul simply, or whether every man severally had his soul given to him by God, even as Adam himself had, without propagation, although he declared, for all that, his conviction that the soul was in its nature spirit, not body, Victor was equally offended with both statements: he wondered that so great a man as Augustin did not unhesitatingly teach what one ought to hold concerning the origin of the soul, especially as he thought its propagation probable; and also that he did state with so great assurance the nature of the soul to be incorporeal. He accordingly published two books written to one Peter, a presbyter of Spain, against Augustin on this subject, containing some conceits of the Pelagian heretics, and other things even worse than these.

A monk called Renatus happened then to be at Cæsarea. It appears that this man had shown to Augustin, who was staying at the same place in the autumn of the year 418, a letter of the Bishop Optatus consulting him about the origin of the soul. This monk, of the order of laymen, but perfectly orthodox in the faith, induced by the circumstance, carefully copied the books of Victor, and forwarded them from Cæsarea to Hippo the next summer; Augustin, however, only received them at the end of autumn of the year 419, as is supposed. As soon as the holy doctor read them, he without delay wrote the first of the four following books to the good monk, and then the second, in the shape of a letter, to the presbyter Peter, and the two last books to Victor himself, but after a considerable interval, as it appears from the following words of the fourth chapter of the second book: "If, indeed, the Lord will that I should write to the young man, as I desire to do." In the Retractations this little work of Augustin is placed immediately after the treatises of the year 419, i.e. in the fifth place after the Proceedings with Emeritus, which were completed in the month of September in the year 418. It belongs, therefore, to the termination of the year 419 or to the commencement of the year 420, having been written after "the condemnation of the Pelagians by the authority of catholic Councils and of the Apostolic See," but "very soon after," as that happy event had happened in the year of Christ 418.

In Book I., written to Renatus, he points out his own opinion about the nature of the soul, and his hesitation as to its origin, which had been unjustly blamed by Victor. He reproves the man's juvenile forwardness, shows him he had fallen into grave and unheard-of errors while venturing to take upon himself the solution of a question which exceeded his abilities, and points out that he adduced only doubtful passages of Scripture, and such as were not applicable to the subject, in his endeavor to prove that souls are not propagated, but that entirely new ones are breathed by God into every man at his separate birth.

In Book II., he advises Peter not to incur the imputation of having approved of the books which had been addressed to him by Victor On the Origin of the Soul by any use he might make of them, nor to take as catholic doctrines that person's rash utterances contrary to the Christian faith. Victor's various and very serious errors he points out and briefly confutes, and he concludes with advising Peter himself to try to persuade Victor to correct his errors.

In Book III., which was written to Victor himself, he points out the corrections which Victor ought to make in his books if he wished to be deemed a catholic; those opinions also and paradoxes of his, which had been already refuted in the preceding books to Renatus and Peter, the author briefly censures in this third book, and classifies under eleven heads of error.

In Book IV., addressed to the same Victor, he first shows that his hesitation about the origin of souls was undeservedly blamed, and that he was wrongly compared with cattle, because he had refrained from any bold conclusions on the subject. Then again, about his own unhesitating statement, that the soul was spirit, not body, he points out how rashly Victor disapproved of this assertion, especially when he was vainly expending his efforts to prove that the soul was corporeal in its own nature, and that the spirit in man was distinct from the soul itself.

A TREATISE ON THE SOUL AND ITS ORIGIN,

BY AURELIUS AUGUSTIN, BISHOP OF HIPPO;

In Four Books,

written towards the end of 419.

Book I.

ADDRESSED TO RENATUS, THE MONK.

On receiving from Renatus the two books of Vincentius Victor, who disapproved of Augustin's opinion touching the nature of the soul, and of his hesitation in respect of its origin, Augustin points out how the young objector, in his self-conceit in aiming to decide on so abstruse a subject, had fallen into insufferable mistakes. He then proceeds to show that those passages of Scripture by which Victor thought he could prove that human souls are not derived by propagation, but are breathed by God afresh into each man at birth, are ambiguous, and inadequate for the confirmation of this opinion of his.

Chapter 1 [I.]—Renatus Had Done Him a Kindness by Sending Him the Books Which Had Been Addressed to Him.

Your sincerity towards us, dearest brother Renatus, and your brotherly kindness, and the affection of mutual love between us, we already had clear proof of; but now you have afforded us a still clearer proof, by sending me two books, written by a person whom I knew, indeed, nothing of,—though he was not on that account to be despised,—called Vincentius Victor (for in such form did I find his name placed at the head of his work): this you did in the summer of last year; but owing to my absence from home, it was the end of autumn before they found their way to me. How, indeed, would you be likely with your very great affection for me to fail either in means or inclination to bring under my notice any writings of the kind, by whomsoever composed, if they fell into your hands, even if they were addressed to someone else? How much less likely, when my own name was mentioned and read—and that in a context of gainsaying some words of mine, which I had published in certain little treatises? Now you have done all this in the way you were sure to act as my very sincere and beloved friend.

Chapter 2 [II.]—He Receives with a Kindly and Patient Feeling the Books of a Young and Inexperienced Man Who Wrote Against Him in a Tone of Arrogance. Vincentius Victor Converted from the Sect of the Rogatians.

I am somewhat pained, however, at being thus far less understood by your Holiness than I should like to be; forasmuch as you supposed that I should so receive your communication, as if you did me an injury, by making known to me what another had done. You may see, indeed, how far this feeling is from my mind, in that I have no complaint to make of having suffered any wrong even from him. For, when he entertained views different from my own, was he bound to preserve silence? It ought, no doubt, to be even pleasant to me, that he broke silence in such a way as to put it in our power to read what he had to say. He ought, I certainly think, to have written simply to me, rather than to another concerning me; but as he was unknown to me, he did not venture to intrude personally on me in refuting my words. He thought there was no necessity for applying to me in a matter on which he seemed to himself least of all liable to be doubted, but to be holding a perfectly well known and certain opinion. He moreover, acted in obedience to a friend of his by whom he tells us he was compelled to write. And if he expressed any sentiment during the controversy which was contumelious to me, I would prefer supposing that he did this, not with any wish to treat me with incivility, but from the necessity of thinking differently from me. For in all cases where a person's animus towards one is indeterminate and unknown, I think it better to suppose the existence of the kindlier motive, than to find fault with an undiscovered one. Perhaps, too, he acted from love to me, as knowing that what he had written might possibly reach me; being at the same time unwilling that I should be in error on such points as he especially thinks himself to be free from error regarding. I ought, therefore, to be grateful for his kindness, although I feel obliged to disapprove of his opinion. Accordingly, about the points on which he does not entertain right views, he appears to me to deserve gentle correction rather than severe disapproval; more especially because, if I am rightly informed, he has lately become a catholic—a matter in which he is to be congratulated. For he has freed himself from the schism and errors of the Donatists (or rather the Rogatists) in which he was previously implicated; and if he understands the catholic verity as he ought, we may really rejoice at his conversion.

Chapter 3 [III]—The Eloquence of Vincentius, Its Dangers and Its Tolerableness.

For he has an eloquence by which he can explain what he thinks. He must, therefore, be dealt with accordingly; and we must hope that he may entertain right sentiments, and that he may not turn useless things into objects of desire; that he may not seem to have propounded as true whatever he may have expressed with eloquence. But in his very outspokenness he may have much to correct, and to prune of redundant verbiage. And this characteristic of his has actually given offence to you, who are a person of gravity, as your own writings indicate. This fault, however, is either easily corrected, or, if it be resorted to with fondness by light minds, and borne with by serious ones, it is not attended with any injury to their faith. For we have already amongst us men who are frothy in speech, but sound in the faith. We need not then despair that this quality even in him (it might be endurable, however, even if it proved permanent) may be tempered and cleansed—in fact, may be either extended or recalled to an entire and solid criterion; especially as he is said to be young, so that diligence may supply to him whatever defect his inexperience may possess, and ripeness of age may digest what crude loquacity finds indigestible. The troublesome, dangerous, and pernicious thing is, when folly is set off by the commendation which is accorded to eloquence, and when a poisonous draught is drunk out of a precious goblet.

Chapter 4 [IV.]—The Errors Contained in the Books of Vincentius Victor. He Says that the Soul Comes from God, But Was Not Made Either Out of Nothing or Out of Any Created Thing.

I will now proceed to point out what things are chiefly to be avoided in his contentious statement. He says that the soul was made, indeed, by God, but that it is not a portion of God or of the nature of God, —which is an entirely true statement. When, however, he refuses to allow that it is made out of nothing, and mentions no other created thing out of which it was made; and makes God its author, in such a sense that He must be supposed to have made it, neither out of any non-existing things, that is, out of nothing, nor out of anything which exists other than God, but out of His very self: he is little aware that in the revolution of his thoughts he has come back to the position which he thinks he has avoided, even that the soul is nothing else than the nature of God; and consequently that there is an actual something made out of the nature of God by the self-same God, for the making of which the material of which He makes it is His own very self who makes it; and that thus God's nature is changeable, and by being changed for the worse the very nature of God Himself incurs condemnation at the hands of the self-same God! How far all this is from being fit for your intelligent faith to suppose, how alien it is from the heart of a catholic, and how much to be avoided, you can readily see. For the soul is either so made from the breath, or God's breath is so made into it, that it was not created out of Himself, but by Himself out of nothing. It is not, indeed, like the case of a human being, when he breathes:

he cannot form a breath out of nothing, but he restores to the air the breath which he inhaled out of it. We may in some such manner suppose that certain airs surrounded the Divine Being, and that He inhaled a particle of it by breathing, and exhaled it again by respiration, when He breathed into man's face, and so formed for him a soul. If this were the process, it could not have been out of His very self, but out of the circumambient airy matter, that what He breathed forth must have arisen. Far be it, however, from us to say, that the Almighty could not have made the breath of life out of nothing, by which man might become a living soul; and to crowd ourselves into such straits, as that we must either think that something already existed other than Himself, out of which He formed breath, or else suppose that He formed out of Himself that which we see was made subject to change. Now, whatever is out of Himself, must necessarily be of the self-same nature as Himself, and therefore immutable: but the soul (as all allow) is mutable. Therefore, it is not out of Him, because it is not immutable, as He is. If, however, it was not made of anything else, it was undoubtedly made out of nothing—but by Himself.

Chapter 5 [V.]—Another of Victor's Errors, that the Soul is Corporeal.

But about his contention, "that the soul is not spirit, but body," what else can he mean to make out, than that we are composed, not of soul and body, but of two or even three bodies? For since he says that we consist of spirit, soul and body, and asserts that all the three are bodies; it follows, that he supposes us to be made up of three bodies. How absurd this conclusion is, I think ought rather to be demonstrated to him than to you. But this is not an intolerable error on the part of a person who has not yet discovered that there is in existence a something, which, though it be not corporeal, yet may wear somewhat of the similitude of a body.

Chapter 6 [VI.]—Another Error Out of His Second Book, to the Effect, that the Soul Deserved to Be Polluted by the Body.

But he is plainly past endurance in what he says in his second book, when he endeavors to solve a very difficult question on original sin, how it belongs to body and soul, if the soul is not derived by parental descent but is breathed afresh by God into a man. Striving to explain this troublesome and profound point, he thus expresses his view: "Through the flesh the soul fitly recovers its primitive condition, which it seemed to have gradually lost through the flesh, in order that it may begin to be regenerated by the very flesh by which it had deserved to be polluted." You observe how this person, having been so bold as to undertake what exceeds his powers, has fallen down such a precipice as to say, that the soul deserved to be defiled by the body; although he could in no wise declare whence it drew on itself this desert, before it put on flesh. For if it first had from the flesh its desert of sin, let him tell us (if he can) whence (before sin) it derived its desert to be contaminated by the flesh. For this desert, which projected it into sinful flesh to be polluted by it, it of course had either from itself, or, which is much more offensive to our mind, from God. It certainly could not, before its being invested with the flesh, have received from that flesh that ill desert because of which it was projected into the flesh, in order to be defiled by it. Now, if it had the ill desert from its own self, how did it get it, seeing that it did no sin before its assumption of flesh? But if it be alleged that it had the ill desert from God, then, I ask, who could listen to such blasphemy? Who could endure it? Who could permit it to be alleged with impunity? For the question which arises here, remember, is not, what was the ill desert which adjudged the soul to be condemned after it became incarnate, but what was its ill desert prior to the flesh, which condemned it to the investiture of the flesh, that it might be thereby polluted? Let him explain this to us, if he can, seeing that he has dared to say that the soul deserved to be defiled by the flesh.

Chapter 7 [VII.]—Victor Entangles Himself in an Exceedingly Difficult Question. God's Foreknowledge is No Cause of Sin.

In another passage, also, on proposing for explanation the very same question in which he had entangled himself, he says, speaking in the person of certain objectors: "Why, they ask, did God inflict upon the soul so unjust a punishment as to be willing to relegate it into a body, when, because of its association with the flesh, that begins to be sinful which could not have been sinful?" Now, amidst the reefy sea of such a question, it was surely his duty to beware of shipwreck; nor to commit himself to dangers which he could not hope to escape by passing over them, and where his only chance of safety lay in putting back again—in a word, by repentance. He tries to free himself by means of the foreknowledge of God, but to no purpose. For God's foreknowledge only marks beforehand those sinners whom He purposes to heal. For if He liberates from sin those souls which He Himself involved in sin when innocent and pure, He then heals a wound which Himself inflicted on us, not which He found in us. May God, however, forbid it, and may it be altogether far from us to say, that when God cleanses the souls of infants by the laver of regeneration, He then corrects evils which He Himself made for them, when He commingled them, which had no sin before, with sinful flesh, that they might be contaminated by its original sin. About, however, the souls which this calumniator alleges to have deserved pollution by the flesh, he is quite unable to tell us how it is they deserved so vast an evil, before their connection with the flesh.

Chapter 8 [VIII.]—Victor's Erroneous Opinion, that the Soul Deserved to Become Sinful.

Vainly supposing, then, that he could solve this question from the foreknowledge of God, he keeps floundering on, and says: "If the soul deserved to be sinful which could not have been sinful, yet neither did it remain in sin, because, as prefigured in Christ, it was not bound to be in sin, even as it was unable to be." Now what can he mean when he says, "which could not have been sinful," or "was unable to be in sin," except, as I suppose, this, if it did not come into the flesh? For, of course, it could not have been sinful through original sin, or have been at all involved in original sin, except through the flesh, if it is not derived from the parent. We see it, then, liberated from sin through grace, but we do not see how it deserved to be involved in sin. What, then, is the meaning of these words of his, "If the soul deserved to be sinful, yet neither did it remain in sin"? For if I were to ask him, why it did not remain in sin, he would very properly answer, Because the grace of Christ delivered it therefrom. Since, then, he tells us how it came to pass that an infant's soul was liberated from its sinfulness, let him further tell us how it happened that it deserved to be sinful.

Chapter 9. —Victor Utterly Unable to Explain How the Sinless Soul Deserved to Be Made Sinful.

But what does he mean by that, which in his introduction he says has befallen him? For before proposing that question of his, and as introducing it, he affirms: "There are other opprobrious expressions underlying the querulous murmurings of those who rail at us; and, shaken about as in a hurricane, we are again and again dashed amongst enormous rocks." Now, if I were to express myself about him in this style, he would probably be angry. The words are his; and after premising them, he propounded his question, by way of showing us the very rocks against which he struck and was wrecked. For to such lengths was he carried, and against such frightful reefs was he borne, drifted, and struck, that his escape was a perfect impossibility without a retreat—a correction, in short, of what he had said; since he was unable to show by what desert the soul was made sinful; though he was not afraid to say, that before any sin of its own it had deserved to become sinful. Now, who deserves, without committing any sin, so immense a punishment as to be conceived in the sin of another, before leaving his mother's womb, and then to be no longer free from sin? But from this punishment the free grace of God delivers the souls of such infants as are regenerated in Christ, with no previous merits of their own—otherwise grace is no grace." With regard, then, to this person, who is so vastly intelligent, and who in the great depth of his wisdom is displeased at our hesitation, which, if not well informed, is at all events circumspect, let him tell us, if he can, what the merit was which brought the soul into such a punishment, from which grace delivers it without any merit. Let him speak, and, if he can, defend his assertion with some show of reason. I would not, indeed, require so much of him, if he had not himself declared that the soul deserved to become sinful. Let him tell us what the desert was—whether good desert or evil? If good, how could well-deserving lead to evil? If evil, whence could arise any ill desert before the commission of any sin? I have also to remark, that if there be a good desert, then the liberation of the soul would not be of free grace, but it would be due to the previous merit, and thus "grace would be no more grace." If there be, however, an evil desert, then I ask what it is. Is it true that the soul has come into the flesh; and that it would not have so come unless He in whom there is no sin had Himself sent it? Never, therefore, except by floundering worse and worse, will he contrive to set up this view of his, in which he predicates of the soul that it deserved to be sinful. In the case of those infants, too, in whose baptism original sin is washed away, he found something to say after a fashion, —to the effect, that being involved in the sin of another could not possibly have been detrimental to them, predestinated as they were to eternal life in the foreknowledge of God. This might admit of a tolerably good sense, if he had not entangled himself in that formula of his, in which he asserts that the soul deserved to be sinful: from this difficulty he can only extricate himself by revoking his words, with regret at having expressed them.

Chapter 10 [IX.]—Another Error of Victor's, that Infants Dying Unbaptized May Attain to the Kingdom of Heaven. Another, that the Sacrifice of the Body of Christ Must Be Offered for Infants Who Die Before They are Baptized.

But when he wished to answer with respect, however, to those infants who are prevented by death from being first baptized in Christ, he was so bold as to promise them not only paradise, but also the kingdom of heaven, —finding no way else of avoiding the necessity of saying that God condemns to eternal death innocent souls which, without any previous desert of sin, He introduces into sinful flesh. He saw, however, to some extent what evil he was giving utterance to, in implying that without any grace of Christ the souls of infants are redeemed to everlasting life and the kingdom of heaven, and that in their case original sin may be cancelled without Christ's baptism, in which is effected the forgiveness of sins: observing all this, and into what a depth he had plunged in his sea of shipwreck, he says, "I am of opinion that for them, indeed, constant oblations and sacrifices must be continually offered up by holy priests." You may here behold another danger, out of which he will never escape except by regret and a recall of his words. For who can offer up the body of Christ for any except for those who are members of Christ? Moreover, from the time when He said, "Except a man be born of water and of the Spirit, he cannot enter into the kingdom of heaven;" and again, "He that loses his life for my sake shall find it;" no one becomes a member of Christ except it be either by baptism in Christ, or death for Christ.

Chapter 11. —Martyrdom for Christ Supplies the Place of Baptism. The Faith of the Thief Who Was Crucified Along with Christ Taken as Martyrdom and Hence for Baptism.

Accordingly, the thief, who was no follower of the Lord before the cross, but His confessor upon the cross, from whose case a presumption is sometimes taken, or attempted, against the sacrament of baptism, is reckoned by St. Cyprian among the martyrs who are baptized in their own blood, as happens to many unbaptized persons in times of hot persecution. For to the fact that he confessed the crucified Lord so much weight is attributed and so much availing value assigned by Him who knows how to weigh and value such evidence, as if he had been crucified for the Lord. Then, indeed, his faith on the cross flourished when that of the disciples failed, and that without recovery if it had not bloomed again by the resurrection of Him before the terror of whose death it had drooped. They despaired of Him when dying, —he hoped when joined with Him in dying; they fled from the author of life, —he prayed to his companion in punishment; they grieved as for the death of a man, —he believed that after death He was to be a king; they forsook the sponsor of their salvation, —he honored the companion of His cross. There was discovered in him the full measure of a martyr, who then believed in Christ when they fell away who were destined to be martyrs. All this, indeed, was manifest to the eyes of the Lord, who at once bestowed so great felicity on one who, though not baptized, was yet washed clean in the blood, as it were, of martyrdom. But even of ourselves, who cannot reflect with how much faith, how much hope, how much charity he might have undergone death for Christ when living, who begged life of Him when dying? Besides all this, there is the circumstance, which is not incredibly reported, that the thief who then believed as he hung by the side of the crucified Lord was sprinkled, as in a most sacred baptism, with the water which issued from the wound of the Savior's side. I say nothing of the fact that nobody can prove, since none of us knows that he had not been baptized before his condemnation. However, let every man take this in the sense he may prefer; only let no rule about baptism affecting the Savior's own precept be taken from this example of the thief; and let no one promise for the case of unbaptized infants, between damnation and the kingdom of heaven, some middle place of rest and happiness, such as he pleases and where he pleases. For this is what the heresy of Pelagius promised them: he neither fears damnation for infants, whom he does not regard as having any original sin, nor does he give them the hope of the kingdom of heaven, since they do not approach to the sacrament of baptism. As for this man, however, although he acknowledges that infants are involved in original sin, he yet boldly promises them, even without baptism, the kingdom of heaven. This even the Pelagians had not the boldness to do, though asserting infants to be absolutely without sin. See, then, what a network of presumptuous opinion he entangles, unless he regrets having committed such views to writing.

Chapter 12 [X.]—Dinocrates, Brother of the Martyr St. Perpetua, is Said to Have Been Delivered from the State of Condemnation by the Prayers of the Saint.

Concerning Dinocrates, however, the brother of St. Perpetua, there is no record in the canonical Scripture; nor does the saint herself, or whoever it was that wrote the account, say that the boy, who had died at the age of seven years, died without baptism; in his behalf she is believed to have had, when her martyrdom was imminent, her prayers effectually heard that he should be removed from the penalties of the lost to rest. Now, boys at that time of life are able both to lie, and, saying the truth, both to confess and deny. Therefore, when they are baptized they say the Creed, and answer in their behalf to such questions as are proposed to them in examination. Who can tell, then, whether that boy, after baptism, in a time of persecution was estranged from Christ to idolatry by an impious father, and on that account incurred mortal condemnation, from which he was only delivered for Christ's sake, given to the prayers of his sister when she was at the point of death?

Chapter 13 [XI.]—The Sacrifice of the Body and Blood of Christ Will Not Avail for Unbaptized Persons, and Can Not Be Offered for the Majority of Those Who Die Unbaptized.

But even if it be conceded to this man (what cannot by any means be allowed with safety to the catholic faith and the rule of the Church), that the sacrifice of the body and blood of Christ may be offered for unbaptized persons of every age, as if they were to be helped by this kind of piety on the part of their friends to reaching the kingdom of heaven: what will he have to say to our objections respecting the thousands of infants who are born of impious parents and never fall, by any mercy of God or man, into the hands of pious friends, and who depart from that wretched life of theirs at their most tender age without the washing of regeneration? Let him tell us, if he only can, how it is that those souls deserved to be made sinful to such a degree as certainly never afterwards to be delivered from sin. For if I ask him why they deserve to be condemned if they are not baptized, he will rightly answer me: Because original sin. If I then inquire whence they derived original sin, he will answer, From sinful flesh, of course. If I go on to ask why they deserved to be condemned to a sinful flesh, seeing they had done no evil before they came in the flesh, and to be so condemned to undergo the contagion of the sin of another, that neither baptism shall regenerate them, born as they are in sin, nor sacrifices expiate them in their pollution: let him find something to reply to this! For in such circumstances and of such parents have these infants been born, or are still being born, that it is not possible for them to be reached with such help. Here, at any rate, all argument is lacking. Our question is not, why souls have deserved to be condemned subsequently to their consorting with sinful flesh? But we ask, how it is that souls have deserved to be condemned to undergo at all this association with sinful flesh, seeing that they have no sin before this association. There is no room for him to say: "It was no detriment to them that they shared for a season the contagion of another's sin, since in the prescience of God redemption had been provided for them." For we are now speaking of those to whom no redemption brings help, since they depart from the body before they are baptized. Nor is there any propriety in his saying: "The souls which baptism does not cleanse, the many sacrifices which are offered up for them will cleanse. God foreknew this, and willed that they should for a little while be implicated in the sins of another without incurring eternal damnation, and with the hope of eternal happiness." For we are now speaking of those whose birth among impious persons and of impious parents could by no possibility find such defenses and helps. And even if these could be applied, they would, it is certain, be unable to benefit any who are unbaptized; just as the sacrifices which he has mentioned out of the book of the Maccabees could be of no use for the sinful dead for whom they were offered, since they had not been circumcised.

Chapter 14.—Victor's Dilemma: He Must Either Say All Infants are Saved, or Else God Slays the Innocent.

Let him, then, find an answer, if he can, when the question is asked of him, why it was that the soul, without any sin whatever, either original or personal, deserved so to be condemned to undergo the original sin of another as to be unable to be delivered from it; let him see which he will choose of two alternatives: Either to say that even the souls of dying infants who depart hence without the washing of regeneration, and for whom no sacrifice of the Lord's body is offered, are absolved from the bond of original sin—although the apostle teaches that "from one all go into condemnation,"—all, that is, of course, to whom grace does not find its way to help, in order that by

One all might escape into redemption. Or else to say that souls which have no sin, either their own or original, and are in every respect innocent, simple, and pure, are punished with eternal damnation by the righteous God when He inserts them Himself into sinful flesh without any deliverance therefrom.

Chapter 15 [XII.]—God Does Not Judge Any One for What He Might Have Done If His Life Had Been Prolonged, But Simply for the Deeds He Actually Commits.

For my own part, indeed, I affirm that neither of the alternative cases ought to be admitted, nor that third opinion which would have it that souls sinned in some other state before the flesh, and so deserved to be condemned to the flesh; for the apostle has most distinctly stated that "the children being not yet born, had done neither good nor evil." So it is evident that infants can have contracted none but original sin to require remission of sins. Nor, again, that fourth position, that the souls of infants who will die without baptism are by the righteous God banished and condemned to sinful flesh, since He foreknew that they would lead evil lives if they grew old enough for the use of free will. But this not even he has been daring enough to affirm, though embarrassed in such perplexities. On the contrary, he has declared, briefly indeed, yet manifestly, against this vain opinion in these words: "God would have been unrighteous if He had willed to judge any man yet unborn, who had done nothing whatever of his own free will." This was his answer when treating a question in opposition to those persons who ask why God made man, when in His foreknowledge He knew that he would not be good? He would be judging a man before he was born if He had been unwilling to create him because He knew beforehand that he would not turn out good. And there can be no doubt about it, even as this person himself thought, that the proper course would be for the Almighty to judge a man for his works when accomplished, not for such as might be foreseen, nor such as might be permitted to be done some time or other. For if the sins which a man would have committed if he were alive are condemned in him when dead, even when they have not been committed, no benefit is conferred on him when he is taken away that no wickedness might change his mind; since judgment will be given upon him according to the wickedness which might have developed in him, not according to the uprightness which was actually found in him. Nor will any man possibly be safe who dies after baptism, because even after baptism men may, I will not say sin in some way or other, but actually go so far as to commit apostasy. What then? Suppose a man who has been taken away after baptism should, if he had lived, have become an apostate, are we to think that no benefit was conferred even upon him in that he was removed and was saved from the misery of his mind being changed by wickedness? And are we to imagine that he will have to be judged, because of God's foreknowledge, as an apostate, and not as a faithful member of Christ? How much better, to be sure, would it have been—if sins are punished not as they have been committed or contemplated by the human agent, but foreknown and to happen in the cognizance of the Almighty—if the first pair had been cast forth from paradise before their fall, and so sin have been prevented in so holy and blessed a place! What, too, is to be said about the entire nullification of foreknowledge itself, when what is foreknown is not to happen? How, indeed, can that be rightly called the prescience of something to be, which in fact will not come to pass? And how are sins punished which are none, that is to say, which are not committed before the assumption of flesh, since life itself is not yet begun; nor after the assumption, since death has prevented?

Chapter 16 [XIII.]—Difficulty in the Opinion Which Maintains that Souls are Not by Propagation.

This means, then, of settling the point whereby the soul was sent into the flesh until what time it should be delivered from the flesh, —seeing that the soul of an infant, which has not grown old enough for the will to become free, is the case supposed, —makes no discovery of the reason why condemnation should overtake it without the reception of baptism, except the reason of original sin. Owing to this sin, we do not deny that the soul is righteously condemned, because for sin God's righteous law has appointed punishment. But then we ask, why the soul has been made to undergo this sinful state, if it is not derived from that one primeval soul which sinned in the first father of the human race. Wherefore, if God does not condemn the innocent,—if He does not make guilty those whom He sees to be innocent,—and if nothing liberates souls from either original sins or personal ones but Christ's baptism in Christ's Church,— and if sins, before they are committed, and much more when they have never been committed, cannot be condemned by any righteous law: then this writer cannot adduce any of these four cases; he must, if he can, explain, in respect to the souls of infants, which, as they quit life without baptism, are sent into condemnation, by what desert of theirs it is that they, without having ever sinned, are consigned to a sinful flesh, there to find the sin which is to secure their just condemnation. Moreover, if he shrinks from these four cases which sound doctrine condemns,—that is to say, if he has not the courage to maintain that souls, when they are even without sin, are made sinful by God, or that they are freed from the original sin that is in them without Christ's sacrament, or that they committed sin in some other state before they were sent into the flesh, or that sins which they never committed are condemned in them,—if, I say, he has not the courage to tell us these things because they really do not deserve to be mentioned but should affirm that infants do not inherit original sin, and have no reason why they should be condemned should they depart hence without receiving the sacrament of regeneration, he will without doubt, to his own condemnation, run into the damnable heresy of Pelagius. To avoid this, how much better is it for him to share my hesitation about the soul's origin, without daring to affirm that which he cannot comprehend by human reason nor defend by divine authority! So shall he not be obliged to utter foolishness, whilst he is afraid to confess his ignorance.

Chapter 17 [XIV.]—He Shows that the Passages of Scripture Adduced by Victor Do Not Prove that Souls are Made by God in Such a Way as Not to Be Derived by Propagation: First Passage.

Here, perhaps, he may say that his opinion is

backed by divine authority, since he supposes that he proves by passages of the Holy Scriptures that souls are not made by God by way of propagation, but that they are by distinct acts of creation breathed afresh into each individual. Let him prove this if he can, and I will allow that I have learnt from him what I was trying to find out with great earnestness. But he must go in quest of other defenses, which, perhaps, he will not find, for he has not proved his point by the passages which he has thus far advanced. For all he has applied to the subject are to some extent undoubtedly suitable, but they afford only doubtful demonstration to the point which he raises respecting the soul's origin. For it is certain that God has given to man breath and spirit, as the prophet testifies: "Thus saith the Lord, who made the heaven, and founded the earth, and all that is therein; who giveth breath to the people upon it, and spirit to them that walk over it." This passage he wishes to be taken in his own sense, which he is defending; so that the words, "who giveth breath to the people," may be understood as implying that He creates souls for people not by propagation, but by insufflation of new souls in every case. Let him, then, boldly maintain at this rate that He does not give us flesh, because our flesh derives its original from our parents. In the instance, too, which the apostle adduces, "God giveth it a body as it hath pleased Him," let him deny, if he dares, that corn springs from corn, and grass from grass, from the seed, each after its kind. And if he dares not deny this, how does he know in what sense it is said, "He giveth breath to the people"? —whether by derivation from parents, or by fresh breathing into each individual?

Chapter 18. —By "Breath" Is Signified Sometimes the Holy Spirit.

How, again, does he know whether the repetition of the idea in the sentence, "who giveth breath to the people upon it, and spirit to them that walk over it," may not be understood of only one thing under two expressions, and may not mean, not the life or spirit whereby human nature lives, but the Holy Spirit? For if by the "breath" the Holy Ghost could not be signified, the Lord would not, when He "breathed upon" His disciples after His resurrection, have said, "Receive ye the Holy Ghost." Nor would it have been thus written in the Acts of the Apostles, "Suddenly there came a sound from heaven, as if a mighty breath were borne in upon them; and there appeared unto them cloven tongues, like as of fire, and it sat upon each of them, and they were all filled with the Holy Ghost." Suppose, now, that it was this which the prophet foretold in the words, "who giveth breath unto the people upon it;" and then, as an exposition of what he had designated "breath," he went on to say, "and spirit to them that walk over it." Surely this prediction was most manifestly fulfilled when they were all filled with the Holy Ghost. If, however, the term "people" is not yet applicable to the one hundred and twenty persons who were then assembled together in one place, at all events, when the number of believers amounted to four or five thousand, who when they were baptized received the Holy Ghost, can any doubt that the recipients of the Holy Ghost were then "the people," even "the men walking in the earth"? For that spirit which is given to man as appertaining to his nature, whether it be given by propagation or be inbreathed as something new to individuals (and I do not determine which of these two modes ought to be affirmed, at least until one of the two can be clearly ascertained beyond a doubt), is not given to men when they "walk over the earth," but whilst they are still shut up in their mother's womb. "He gave breath, therefore, to the people upon the earth, and spirit to them that walk over it," when many became believers together, and were together filled with the Holy Ghost. And He gives Him to His people, although not to all at the same time, but to everyone in His own time, until, by departing from this life, and by coming into it, the entire number of His people be fulfilled. In this passage of Holy Scripture, therefore, breath is not one thing, and spirit another thing; but there is a repetition of one and the same idea. Just as "He that sits in the heavens" is not one, and "the Lord" is not another; nor, again, is it one thing "to laugh," and another thing "to hold in derision;" but there is only a repetition of the same meaning in the passage where we read, "He that sits in the heavens shall laugh: the Lord shall have them in derision." So, in precisely the same manner, in the passage, "I will give Thee the heathen for Thine inheritance, and the uttermost parts of the earth for Thy possession," it is certainly not meant that "inheritance" is one thing, and "possession" another thing; nor that "the heathen" means one thing, and "the uttermost parts of the earth" another; there is only a repetition of the self-same thing. He will, indeed, discover innumerable expressions of this sort in the sacred writings, if he will only attentively consider what he reads.

Chapter 19. —The Meaning of "Breath" In Scripture.

The term, however, that is used in the Greek version, πνoή, is variously rendered in Latin: sometimes by flatus, breath; sometimes by spiritus, spirit; sometimes by inspiratio, inspiration. This term occurs in the Greek editions of the passage which we are now reviewing, "Who giveth breath to the people upon it," the word for breath being πνoή. The same word is used in the narrative where man was endued with life: "And God breathed upon his face the breath of life." Again, in the psalm the same term occurs: "Let everything that hath spirit praise the Lord." It is the same word also in the Book of Job: "The inspiration of the Almighty is that which teaches." The translator refused the word flatus, breath, for adspiratio, inspiration, although he had before him the very term πνoή, which occurs in the text of the prophet which we are considering. We can hardly doubt, I think, that in this passage of Job the Holy Ghost is signified. The question discussed was concerning wisdom, whence it comes to men: "It cometh not from number of years; but the Spirit is in mortals, and the inspiration of the Almighty is that which teaches." By this repetition of terms it may be quite understood that he did not speak of man's own spirit in the clause, "The Spirit is in mortals." He wanted to show whence men have wisdom, —that it is not from their own selves; so by using a duplicate expression he explains his idea; "The inspiration of the Almighty is that which teaches." Similarly, in another passage of the same book, he says, "The understanding of my lips shall meditate purity. The divine Spirit is that which formed me, and the breath of the Almighty is that which teaches me." Here, likewise, what he calls adspiratio, or "inspiration," is in Greek πνοή, the same word which is translated flatus, "breath," in the passage quoted from the prophet. Therefore, although it is rash to deny that the passage, "Who giveth breath to the people upon it, and spirit to them that walk over it," has reference to the soul or spirit of man,— although the Holy Ghost may with greater credibility be understood as referred to in the passage: yet I ask on what ground anybody can boldly determine that the prophet meant in these words to intimate that the soul or spirit whereby our nature possesses vitality [is not given to us by God through the process of propagation?] Of course if the prophet had very plainly said, "Who giveth soul to the people upon earth," it still would remain to be asked whether God Himself gives it from an origin in the preceding generation, just as He gives the body out of such prior material, and that not only to men or cattle, but also to the seed of corn, or to any other body whatever, just as it pleases Him; or whether He bestows it by inbreathing as a new gift to each individual, as the first man received it from Him?

Chapter 20. —Other Ways of Taking the Passage.

There are also some persons who understand the prophet's words, "He gave breath to the people upon it," that is to say, upon the earth, as if the word "breath," flatus, were simply equivalent to "soul," anima; while they construe the next clause, "and spirit to them that walk over it," as referring to the Holy Ghost; and they suppose that the same order is observed by the prophet that is mentioned by the apostle: "That was not first which is spiritual, but that which is natural; and afterward that which is spiritual." Now from this view of the prophet's words an elegant interpretation may, no doubt, be formed consistent with the apostle's sense. The phrase, "to them that walk over it," is in the Latin, "calcantibus eam;" and as the literal meaning of these words is "treading upon it," we may understand the idea of contempt of it to be implied. For they who receive the Holy Ghost despise earthly things in their love of heavenly things. None of these opinions, however, is contrary to the faith, whether one regards the two terms, breath and spirit, to pertain to human nature, or both of them to the Holy Ghost, or one of them, breath, to the soul, and the other, spirit, to the Holy Ghost. If, however, the soul and spirit of the human being be the meaning here, since undoubtedly it ought to be, as the gift of God to him, then we must further inquire, in what way does God bestow this gift? Is it by propagation, as He gives us our bodily limbs by this process? Or is it bestowed on each person severally by God's inbreathing, not by propagation, but as always a fresh creation? These questions are not ambiguous, as this man would make them; but we wish that they be defended by the most certain warrant of the divine Scriptures.

Chapter 21. —The Second Passage Quoted by Victor.

On the same principle we treat the passage in which God says: "For my Spirit shall go forth from me; and I have created every breath." Here the former clause, "My Spirit shall go forth from me, must be taken as referring to the Holy Ghost, of whom the Savior similarly says, "He proceeded from the Father." But the other clause, "I have created every breath," is undeniably spoken of each individual soul. Well; but God also creates the entire body of man; and, as nobody doubts, He makes the human body by the process of propagation: it is therefore, of course, still open to inquiry concerning the soul (since it is evidently God's work), whether He creates it as He does the body; by propagation, or by inbreathing, as He made the first soul.

Chapter 22. —Victor's Third Quotation.

He proceeds to favor us with a third passage, in which it is written: "Who forms the spirit of man within him." As if anyone denied this! No; all our question is as to the mode of the formation. Now let us take the eye of the body, and ask, who but God forms it? I suppose that He forms it not externally, but in itself, and yet, most certainly, by propagation. Since, then, He also forms "the human spirit in him," the question still remains, whether it be derived by a fresh insufflation in every instance, or by propagation.

Chapter 23. —His Fourth Quotation.

We have read all about the mother of the Maccabean youths, who was really more fruitful in virtues when her children suffered than of children when they were born; how she exhorted them to constancy, speaking in this wise: "I cannot tell, my sons, how ye came into my womb. For it was not I who gave you spirit and soul, nor was it I that formed the members of every one of you; but it was God, who also made the world, and all things that are therein; who, moreover, formed the generation of men; and searches the action of all; and who will Himself of His great mercy restore to you your spirit and soul." All this we know; but how it supports this man's assertion we do not see. For what Christian would deny that God gives to men soul and spirit? But similarly, I suppose that he cannot deny that God gives to men their tongue, and ear, and hand, and foot, and all their bodily sensations, and the form and nature of all their limbs. For how is he going to deny all these to be the gifts of God, unless he forgets that he is a Christian? As, however, it is evident that these were made by Him, and bestowed on man by propagation; so also the question must arise, by what means man's spirit and soul are formed by Him; by what efficiency given to man—from the parents, or from nothing, or (as this man asserts, in a sense which we must by all means guard against) from some existing nature of the divine breath, not created out of nothing, but out of His own self?

Chapter 24 [XV.]—Whether or No the Soul is Derived by Natural Descent (Ex Traduce), His Cited Passages Fail to Show.

Forasmuch, then, as the passages of Scripture which he mentions by no means show what he endeavors to enforce (since, indeed, they express nothing at all on the immediate question before us), what can be the meaning of these words of his: "We firmly maintain that the soul comes from the breath of God, not from natural generation, because it is given from God"? As if, forsooth, the body could be given from another, than from Him by whom it is created, "Of whom are all things, through whom are all things, in whom are all things;" not that they are of His nature, but of His workmanship. "Nor is it from nothing," says he, "because it comes forth from God." Whether this be so, is (we must say) not the question to be here entertained. At the same time, we do not hesitate to affirm, that the proposition which he advances, that the soul comes to man neither out of descent nor out of nothing, is certainly not true: this, I say, we affirm to be without doubt not true. For it is one of two things: if the soul is not derived by natural descent from the parent, it comes out of nothing. To pretend that it is derived from God in such wise as to be a portion of His nature, is simply sacrilegious blasphemy. But we solicit and seek up to the present time some plain passages of Scripture bearing on the point, whether the soul does not come by parental descent; but we do not want such passages as he has adduced, which yield no illustration of the question now before us.

Chapter 25. —Just as the Mother Knows Not Whence Comes Her Child Within Her, So We Know Not Whence Comes the Soul.

How I wish that, on so profound a question, so long as he is ignorant what he should say, he would imitate the mother of the Maccabean youths! Although she knew very well that she had conceived children of her husband, and that they had been created for her by the Creator of all, both in body and in soul and spirit, yet she says, "I cannot tell, my sons, how ye came into my womb." Well now, I only wish this man would tell us that which she was ignorant of! She, of course, knew (on the points I have mentioned) how they came into her womb as to their bodily substance, because she could not possibly doubt that she had conceived them by her husband. She furthermore confessed—because this, too, she was, of course, well aware of—that it was God who gave them their soul and spirit, and that it was He also who formed for them their features and their limbs. What was it, then, that she was so ignorant of? Was it not probably (what we likewise are equally unable to determine) whether the soul and spirit, which God no doubt bestowed upon them, was derived to them from their parents, or breathed into them separately as it had been into the first man? But whether it was this, or some other particular respecting the constitution of human nature, of which she was ignorant, she frankly confessed her ignorance; and did not venture to defend at random what she knew nothing about. Nor would this man say to her, what he has not been ashamed to say to us: "Man being in honor doth not understand; he is compared to the senseless cattle, and is like unto them." Behold how that woman said of her sons, "I cannot tell how ye came into my womb," and yet she is not compared to the senseless brutes. "I cannot tell," she said; then, as if they would inquire of her why she was ignorant, she went on to say, "For it was not I who gave you spirit and soul." He, therefore, who gave them that gift, knows whence He made what He gave, whether He communicated it by propagation, or breathed it as a fresh creation, —a point which (this man says) I for my part know nothing of. "Nor was it I that formed the features and members of every one of you." He, however, who formed them, knows whether He formed them with the soul, or gave the soul to them after they had been formed. She had no idea of the manner, this or that, in which her sons came into her womb; only one thing was she sure of, that He who gave her all she had would restore to her what He gave. But this man would choose out what that woman was ignorant of, on so profound and abstruse a fact of our nature; only he would not judge her, if in error; nor compare her, if ignorant, to the senseless cattle. Whatever the point was about which she was ignorant, it certainly pertained to man's nature; and yet anybody would be blameless for such ignorance. Wherefore, I too, on my side, say concerning my soul, I have no certain knowledge how it came into my body; for it was not I who gave it to myself. He who gave it to me knows whether He imparted it to me from my father, or created it afresh for me, as He did for the first man. But even I shall know, when He Himself shall teach me, in His own good time. Now, however, I do not know; nor am I ashamed, like him, to confess my ignorance of what I know not.

Chapter 26 [XVI.]—The Fifth Passage of Scripture Quoted by Victor.

"Learn," says he, "for, behold the apostle teaches you." Yes, indeed, I will learn, if the apostle teaches; since it is God alone who teaches by the apostle. But, pray, what is it which the apostle teaches? "Behold," he adds, "how, when speaking to the men of Athens, he strongly set forth this truth, saying: 'Seeing He giveth to all life and spirit.'" Well, who thinks of denying this? "But understand," he says, "what it is the apostle states: He giveth; not, He hath given. He refers us to continuous and indefinite time, and does not proclaim past and completed time. Now that which he gives without cessation, He is always giving; just as He who gives is

Himself ever existent." I have quoted his words precisely as I found them in the second of the books which you sent me. First, I beg you to notice to what lengths he has gone, while endeavoring to affirm what he knows nothing about. For he has dared to say, that God, without any cessation, and not merely in the present time, but for ever and ever, gives souls to persons when they are born. "He is always giving," says he, "just as He who gives is Himself ever existent." Far be it from me to say that I do not understand what the apostle said, for it is plain enough. But what this man says, he even ought himself to know, is contrary to the Christian faith; and he should be on his guard against going any further in such assertions. For, of course, when the dead shall rise again, there will be no more persons to be born; therefore God will bestow no longer any souls at any birth; but those which He is now giving to men along with their bodies He will judge. So that He is not always giving, although He is ever existent, who at present is giving. Nor, indeed, is that at all derivable from the apostle's expression, who giveth (not hath given), which this writer wishes to deduce, namely, that God does not give men souls by propagation. For souls are still given by Him, even if it be by propagation; even as bodily endowments, such as limbs, and sensations, and shape, and, in fact, the whole substance, are given by God Himself to human beings, although it be by propagation that He gives them. Nor again, because the Lord says, "If God so clothes the grass of the field, which to-day is, and to-morrow is cast into the oven" (not using the preterit time, hath clothed, as when He first formed the material; but employing the present form, clothes, which, indeed, He still is doing), shall we on that account say, that the lilies are not produced from the original source of their own kind. What, therefore, if the soul and spirit of a human being in like manner is given by God Himself, whenever it is given; and given, too, by propagation from its own kind? Now this is a position which I neither maintain nor refute. Nevertheless, if it must be defended or confuted, I certainly recommend its being done by clear, and not doubtful proofs. Nor do I deserve to be compared with senseless cattle because I avow myself to be as yet incapable of determining the question, but rather with cautious persons, because I do not recklessly teach what I know nothing about. But I am not disposed on my own part to return railing for railing and compare this man with brutes; but I warn him as a son to acknowledge that he is really ignorant of that which he knows nothing about; nor to attempt to teach that which he has not yet learnt, lest he should deserve to be compared with those persons whom the apostle mentions as "desiring to be teachers of the law, understanding neither what they say nor whereof they affirm."

Chapter 27 [XVII.]—Augustin Did Not Venture to Define Anything About the Propagation of the Soul.

For whence comes it that he is so careless about the Scriptures, which he talks of, as not to notice that when he reads of human beings being from God, it is not merely, as he contends, in respect of their soul and spirit, but also about their body? For the apostle's statement, "We are His offspring," this man supposes must not be referred to the body, but only to the soul and spirit. If, indeed, our human bodies are not of God, then that is false which the Scripture says: "For of Him are all things, through Him are all things, and in Him are all things." Again, with reference to the same apostle's statement, "For as the woman is of the man, so also is the man by the woman," let him explain to us what propagation he would choose to be meant in the process, —that of the soul, or of the body, or of both? But he will not allow that souls come by propagation: it remains, therefore, that, according to him and all who deny the propagation of souls, the apostle signified the masculine and feminine body only, when he said, "As the woman is of the man, so also is the man by the woman;" the woman having been made out of the man, in order that the man might afterwards, by the process of birth, come out of the woman. If, therefore, the apostle, when he said this, did not intend the soul and spirit also to be understood, but only the bodies of the two sexes, why does he immediately add, "But all things are of God," unless it be that bodies also are of God? For so runs his entire statement: "As the woman is of the man, so also is the man by the woman; but all things are of God." Let, then, our disputant determine of what this is said. If of men's bodies, then, of course, even bodies are of God. How comes it to pass, therefore, that whenever this person reads in Scripture the phrase, "of God," when man is in question, he will have the words understood, not about men's bodies, but only as concerning their souls and spirits? But if the expression, "All things are of God," was spoken both of the body of the two sexes, and of their soul and spirit, it follows that in all things the woman is of the man, for the woman comes from the man, and the man is by the woman: but all things of God. What "all things" are meant, except those he was speaking of, namely, the man of whom came the woman, and the woman who was of the man, and also the man who came by the woman? For that man came not by woman, out of whom came the woman; but only he who afterwards was born of man by woman, just as men are now born. Hence it follows that if the apostle, when he said the words we have quoted from him, spoke of men's bodies, undoubtedly the bodies of persons of both sexes are of God. Furthermore, if he insists that nothing in man comes from God except their souls and spirits, then, of course, the woman is of the man even about her soul and spirit; so that nothing is left to those who dispute against the propagation of souls. But if he is for dividing the subject in such a manner as to say that the woman is of the man about her body, but is of God in respect of her soul and spirit, how, then, will that be true which the apostle says, "All things of God," if the woman's body is of the man in such a sense that it is not of God? Wherefore, allowing that the apostle is more likely to speak the truth than that this person must be preferred as an authority to the apostle, the woman is of the man, whether in regard to her body only, or in reference to the entire whole of which human nature consists (but we assert nothing on these points as an absolute certainty, but are still inquiring after their truth); and the man is through the woman, whether it be that his whole nature as man is derived to him from his father, and is born in him through the woman, or the flesh alone; about which points the question is still undecided. "All things, however, are of God," and about this there is no question; and in this phrase are included the body, soul, and spirit, both of the man and the woman. For even if they were not born or derived from God, or emanated from Him as portions of His nature, yet they are of God, since whatever is created, formed, and made by Him, has from Him the reality of its existence.

Chapter 28. —A Natural Figure of Speech Must Not Be Literally Pressed.

He goes on to remark: "But the apostle, by saying, 'And He Himself giveth life and spirit to all,' and then by adding the words, 'And hath made the whole race of men of one blood,' has referred this soul and spirit to the Creator in respect of their origin, and the body to propagation." Now, certainly anyone who does not wish to deny at random the propagation of souls, before ascertaining clearly whether the opinion is correct or not, has ground for understanding, from the apostle's words, that he meant the expression, of one blood, to be equivalent to of one man, by the figure of speech which understands the whole from its part. Well, then, if it be allowable for this man to take the whole from a part in the passage, "And man became a living soul," as if the spirit also was understood to be implied, about which the Scripture there said nothing, why is it not allowable to others to attribute an equally comprehensive sense to the expression, of one blood, so that the soul and spirit may be considered as included in it, on the ground that the human being who is signified by the term "blood" consists not of body alone, but also of soul and spirit? For just as the controversialist who maintains the propagation of souls, ought not, on the one hand, to press this man too hard, because the Scripture says concerning the first man, "In whom all have sinned" (for the expression is not, In whom the flesh of all has sinned, but "all," that is, "all men," seeing that man is not flesh only);—as, I repeat, he ought not to be too hard pressed himself, because it happens to be written "all men," in such a way that they might be understood simply in respect of the flesh; so, on the other hand, he ought not to bear too hard on those who hold the propagation of souls, on the ground of the phrase, "The whole race of men of one blood," as if this passage proved that flesh alone was transmitted by propagation. For if it is true, as they assert, that soul does not descend from soul, but flesh only from flesh, then the expression, "of one blood," does not signify the entire human being, on the principle of a part for the whole, but merely the flesh of one person alone; while that other expression, "In whom all have sinned," must be so understood as to indicate merely the flesh of all men, which has been handed on from the first man, the Scripture signifying a part by the whole. If, on the other hand, it is true that the entire human being is propagated of each man, himself also entire, consisting of body, soul, and spirit, then the passage, "In whom all have sinned," must be taken in its proper literal sense; and the other phrase, "of one blood," is used metaphorically, the whole being signified by a part, that is to say, the whole man who consists of soul and flesh; or rather (as this person is fond of putting it) of soul, and spirit, and flesh. For both modes of expression the Holy Scriptures are in the habit of employing, putting both a part for the whole and the whole for a part. A part, for instance, implies the whole, in the place where it is said, "Unto Thee shall all flesh come;" the whole man being understood by the term flesh. And the whole sometimes implies a part, as when it is said that Christ was buried, whereas it was only His flesh that was buried. Now about the statement which is made in the apostle's testimony, to the effect that "He giveth life and spirit to all," I suppose that nobody, after the foregoing discussion, will be moved by it. No doubt "He giveth;" the fact is not in dispute; our question is, How does He give it? By fresh inbreathing in every instance, or by propagation? For with perfect propriety is He said to give the substance of the flesh to the human being, though at the same time it is not denied that He gives it by means of propagation.

Chapter 29 [XVIII.]—The Sixth Passage of Scripture Quoted by Victor.

Let us now look at the quotation from Genesis, where the woman was created out of the side of the man, and was brought to him, and he said: "This is now bone of my bones, and flesh of my flesh." Our opponent thinks that "Adam ought to have said, 'Soul of my soul, or spirit of my spirit,' if this, too, had been derived from him." But, in fact, they who maintain the opinion of the propagation of souls feel that they possess a more impregnable defense of their position in the fact that in the Scripture narrative which informs us that God took a rib out of the man's side and formed it into a woman, it is not added that He breathed into her face the breath of life; for this reason, as they say, because she had already been ensouled from the man. If, indeed, she had not, they say, the sacred Scripture would certainly not have kept us in ignorance of the circumstance. With regard to the fact that Adam says, "This is now bone of my bone, and flesh of my flesh," without adding, Spirit or soul, from my spirit or soul, they may answer, just as it has been already shown, that the expression, "my flesh and bone," may be understood as indicating the whole by a part, only that the portion that was taken out of man was not dead, but ensouled; for no good ground for denying that the

Almighty was able to do all this is furnished by the circumstance that not a human being could be found capable of cutting off a part of a man's flesh along with the soul. Adam went on, however, to say, "She shall be called woman, because she was taken out of man." Now, why does he not rather say (and thus confirm the opinion of our opponents), "Since her flesh was taken out of man"? As the case stands, indeed, they who hold the opposite view may well contend, from the fact that it is written, not woman's flesh, but the woman herself was taken out of man, that she must be considered in her entire nature endued with soul and spirit. For although the soul is undistinguished by sex, yet when women are mentioned it is not necessary to regard them apart from the soul. On no other principle would they be thus admonished with respect to self-adornment. "Not with braided hair, or gold, or pearls, or costly array; but which (says the apostle) becometh women professing godliness with a good conversation." Now, "godliness," of course, is an inner principle in the soul or spirit; and yet they are called women, although the ornamentation concerns that internal portion of their nature which has no sex.

Chapter 30—The Danger of Arguing from Silence.

Now, while the disputants are thus contending with one another in alternate argument, I so judge between them that they must not rely on uncertain evidence; nor make bold assertions on points of which they are ignorant. For if the Scripture had said, "God breathed into the woman's face the breath of life, and she became a living soul," it would not have followed even then that the human soul is not derived by propagation from parents, except the same statement were likewise made concerning their son. For it might have been that whilst an unensouled member taken from the body might require to be ensouled, yet that the soul of the son might be derived from the father, transfused by propagation through the mother. There is, however, an absolute silence on the point; it is entirely concealed from our view. Nothing is denied, but at the same time nothing is affirmed. And thus, if in any place the Scripture is possibly not quite silent, the point requires to be supported by clearer proofs. Whence it follows, that neither they who maintain the propagation of souls receive any assistance from the circumstance that God did not breathe into the woman's face; nor ought they, who deny this doctrine because Adam did not say, "This is soul of my soul," to persuade themselves to believe what they know nothing of. For just as it has been possible for the Scripture to be silent on the point of the woman's having received her soul, like the man, by the inbreathing of God, without the question before us being solved, but, on the contrary, remaining open; so has it been possible for the same question to remain open and unsolved, notwithstanding the silence of Scripture, as to whether or not Adam said, This is soul of my soul. And hence, if the soul of the first woman comes from the man, a part signifies the whole in his exclamation, "This is now bone of my bones, and flesh of my flesh;" inasmuch as not her flesh alone, but the entire woman, was taken out of man. If, however, it is not from the man, but came by God's inbreathing it into her, as at first into the man, then the whole signifies a part in the passage, "She was taken out of the man;" since on the supposition it was not her whole self, but her flesh that was taken.

Chapter 31. —The Argument of the Apollinarians to Prove that Christ Was Without the Human Soul of This Same Sort.

Although, then, this question remains unsolved by these passages of Scripture, which are certainly indecisive so far as pertains to the point before us, yet I am quite sure of this, that those persons who think that the soul of the first woman did not come from her husband's soul, on the ground of its being only said, "Flesh of my flesh," and not, "Soul of my soul," do, in fact, argue in precisely the same manner as the Apollinarians argue, and all such gainsayers, in opposition to the Lord's human soul, which they deny for no other reason than because they read in the Scripture, "The Word was made flesh." For if, say they, there was a soul in Him also, it ought to have been said, "The Word was made man." But the reason why the great truth is stated in the terms in question really is, that under the designation flesh, Holy Scripture is accustomed to describing the entire human being, as in the passage, "And all flesh shall see the salvation of God." For flesh alone without the soul cannot see anything. Besides, many other passages of the Holy Scriptures go to make it manifest, without any ambiguity, that in the man Christ there is not only flesh, but a human—that is, a reasonable—soul also. Whence they, who maintain the propagation of souls might also understand that a part is put for the whole in the passage, "Bone of my bone, and flesh of my flesh," in such wise that the soul, too, be understood as implied in the words, in the same manner as we believe that the Word became flesh, not without the soul. All that is wanted is, that they should support their opinion of the propagation of souls on passages which are unambiguous; just as other passages of Scripture show us that Christ possesses a human soul. On precisely the same principle we advise the other side also, who do away with the opinion of the propagation of souls, that they should produce certain proofs for their assertion that souls are created by God in every fresh case by insufflation, and that they should then maintain the position that the saying, "This is bone of my bone, and flesh of my flesh," was not spoken figuratively as a part for the whole, including the soul in its signification, but in a bare literal sense of the flesh alone.

Chapter 32 [XIX.]—The Self-Contradiction of Victor as to the Origin of the Soul.

Under these circumstances, I find that this treatise of mine must now be closed. It contains, in fact, all that seemed to me chiefly necessary to the subject under discussion. They who peruse its contents will know how to be on their guard against agreeing with the person whose two books you sent me, so as not to believe with him, that souls are produced by the breath of God in such wise as not to be made out of nothing. The man, indeed, who supposes this, however much he may in words deny the conclusion, does in reality affirm that souls have the substance of God, and are His offspring, not by endowment, but by nature. For from whomsoever a man derives the origin of his nature, from him, in all sober earnestness, it must needs be admitted, that he also derives the kind of his nature. But this author is, after all, self-contradictory: at one time he says that "souls are the offspring of God, —not, indeed, by nature, but by endowment;" and at another time he says, that "they are not made out of nothing, but derive their origin from God." Thus, he does not hesitate to refer them to the nature of God, a position which he had previously denied.

Chapter 33. —Augustin Has No Objection to the Opinion About the Propagation of Souls Being Refuted, and that About Their Insufflation Being Maintained.

As for the opinion, that new souls are created by inbreathing without being propagated, we certainly do not in the least object to its maintenance, —only let it be by persons who have succeeded in discovering some new evidence, either in the canonical Scriptures, in the shape of unambiguous testimony towards the solution of a most knotty question, or else in their own reasonings, such as shall not be opposed to catholic truth, but not by such persons as this man has shown himself to be. Unable to find anything worth saying, and at the same time unwilling to suspend his disputatious propensity, without measuring his strength at all, in order to avoid saying nothing, he boldly affirmed that "the soul deserved to be polluted by the flesh," and that "the soul deserved to become sinful;" though before its incarnation he was unable to discover any merit in it, whether good or evil. Moreover, that "in infants departing from the body without baptism original sin may be remitted, and that the sacrifice of Christ's body must be offered for them," who have not been incorporated into Christ through His sacraments in His Church, and that "they, quitting this present life without the laver of regeneration, not only can go to rest, but can even attain to the kingdom of heaven."

He has propounded a good many other absurdities, which it would be evidently tedious to collect together, and to consider in this treatise. If the doctrine of the propagation of souls is false, may its refutation not be the work of such disputants; and may the defense of the rival principle of the insufflation of new souls in every creative act, proceed from better hands.

Chapter 34. —The Mistakes Which Must Be Avoided by Those Who Say that Men's Souls are Not Derived from Their Parents, But are Afresh Inbreathed by God in Every Instance.

All, therefore, who wish to maintain that new souls are rightly said to be breathed into persons at their birth, and not derived from their parents, must by all means be cautious on each of the four points which I have already mentioned. That is to say, do not let them affirm that souls become sinful by another's original sin; do not let them affirm that infants who died unbaptized can possibly reach eternal life and the kingdom of heaven by the remission of original sin in any other way whatever; do not let them affirm that souls had sinned in some other place previous to their incarnation, and that on this account they were forcibly introduced into sinful flesh; nor let them affirm that the sins which were not actually found in them were, because they were foreknown, deservedly punished, although they were never permitted to reach that life where they could be committed. Provided that they affirm none of these points, because each of them is simply false and impious, they may, if they can, produce any conclusive testimonies of the Holy Scriptures on this question; and they may maintain their own opinion, not only without any prohibition from me, but even with my approbation and best thanks. If, however, they fail to discover any very decided authority on the point in the divine oracles, and are obliged to propound any one of the four opinions because of their failure, let them restrain their imagination, lest they should be driven in their difficulty to enunciate the now damnable and very recently condemned heresy of Pelagius, to the effect that the souls of infants have not original sin. It is, indeed, better for a man to confess his ignorance of what he knows nothing about, than either to run into heresy which has been already condemned, or to found some new heresy, while recklessly daring to defend over and over again opinions which only display his ignorance. This man has made some other absurd mistakes, indeed many, in which he has wandered out of the beaten track of truth, without going, however, to dangerous lengths; and I would like, if the Lord be willing, to write even to himself something about his books; and probably I shall point them all out to him, or a good many of them if I should be unable to notice all.

Chapter 35 [XX.]—Conclusion.

As for this present treatise, which I have thought it proper to address to no other person in preference to yourself, who have taken a kindly and true interest both in our common faith and my character, as a true catholic and a good friend, you will give it to be read or copied by any persons you may be able to find interested in the subject, or may deem worthy to be trusted. In it I have thought proper to repress and confute the presumption of this young man, in such a way, however, as to show that I love him, wishing him to be amended rather than condemned, and to make such progress in the great house which is the catholic Church, whither the divine compassion has conducted him, that he may be therein "a vessel unto honor, sanctified, and meet for the Master's use, and prepared unto every good work," both by holy living and sound teaching. But I have this further to say: if it behooves me to bestow my love upon him, as I sincerely do, how much more ought I to love you, my brother, whose affection towards me and whose catholic faith I have found by the best of proofs to be cautious and sober! The result of your loyalty has been, that you have, with a brother's real love and duty, taken care to have the books, which displeased you, and wherein you found my name treated in a way which ran counter to your liking, copied out and forwarded to me. Now, I am so far from feeling offended at this charitable act of yours, because you did it, that I think I should have had a right, on the true claims of friendship, to have been angry with you if you had not done it. I therefore give you my most earnest thanks. Moreover, I have afforded a still plainer indication of the spirit in which I have accepted your service, by instantly composing this treatise for your consideration, as soon as I had read those books of his.

Book II.

IN THE SHAPE OF A LETTER ADDRESSED TO THE PRESBYTER PETER.

He advises Peter not to incur the imputation of having approved of the books which had been addressed to him by Victor on the origin of the soul, by any use he might make of them, nor to take as Catholic doctrines that person's rash utterances contrary to the Christian faith. Victor's various errors, and those, too, of a very serious character, he points out and briefly confutes; and he concludes with advising Peter himself to try to persuade Victor to amend his errors.

To his Lordship, my dearly beloved brother and fellow-presbyter Peter, Augustin, bishop, sends greeting in the Lord.

Chapter 1 [I.]—Depraved Eloquence an Injurious Accomplishment.

There have reached me the two books of Vincentius Victor, which he addressed in writing to your Holiness; they have been forwarded to me by our brother Renatus, a layman indeed, but a person who has a prudent and religious care about the faith both of himself and of all he loves. On reading these books, I saw that their author was a man of great resources in speech, of which he had enough, and more than enough; but that about which he wished to teach, he was as yet insufficiently instructed. If, however, by the gracious gift of the Lord this qualification were also conferred upon him, he would be serviceable to many. For he possesses in no slight degree the faculty of explaining and beautifying what he thinks; all that is wanted is, that he should first take care to think rightly. Depraved eloquence is a hurtful accomplishment; for to persons of inadequate information it always carries the appearance of truth in its readiness of speech. I know not, indeed, how you received his books; but if I am correctly informed, you are said, after reading them, to have been so greatly overjoyed, that you (though an elderly man and a presbyter) kissed the face of this youthful layman, and thanked him for having taught you what you had been previously ignorant of. Now, in this conduct of yours I do not disapprove of your humility; indeed, I rather commend it; for it was not the man whom you praised, but the truth itself which deigned to speak to you through him: only I wish you were able to point out to me what was the truth which you received through him. I should, therefore, be glad if you would show me, in your answer to this letter, what it was he taught you. Be it far from me to be ashamed to learn from a presbyter, since you did not blush to be instructed by a layman, in proclaiming and imitating your humble conduct, if the lessons were only true in which you received instruction.

Chapter 2 [II.]—He Asks What the Great Knowledge is that Victor Imparts.

Therefore, brother greatly beloved, I desire to know what you learned of him, in order that, if I have already possessed the knowledge, I may participate in your joy; but if I happen to be ignorant, I may be instructed by you. Did you not then understand that there are two somethings, soul and spirit, according as it is said in Scripture, "Thou wilt separate my soul from my spirit"? And that both of them pertain to man's nature, so that the whole man consists of spirit, and soul, and body? Sometimes, however, these two are combined together under the designation of soul; for instance, in the passage, "And man became a living soul." Now, in this place the spirit is implied. Similarly in sundry passages the two are described under the name of spirit, as when it is written,

"And He bowed His head and gave up the spirit;" in which passage it is the soul that must also be understood. And that the two are of one and the same substance? I suppose that you already knew all this. But if you did not, then you may as well know that you have not acquired any great knowledge, the ignorance of which would be attended with much danger. And if there must be any subtler discussion on such points it would be better to carry on the controversy with himself, whose wordy qualities we have already discovered. The questions we might consider are: whether, when mention is made of the soul, the spirit is also implied in the term in such a way that the two comprise the soul, the spirit being, as it were, some part of it,—whether, in fact (as this person seemed to think), under the designation soul, the whole is so designated from only a part; or else, whether the two together make up the spirit, that which is properly called soul being a part thereof; whether again, in fact, the whole is not called from only a part, when the term spirit is used in such a wide sense as to comprehend the soul also, as this man supposes. These, however, are but subtle distinctions, and ignorance about them certainly is not attended with any great danger.

Chapter 3. —The Difference Between the Senses of the Body and Soul.

Again, I wonder whether this man taught you the difference between the bodily senses and the sensibilities of the soul; and whether you, who were a person of considerable age and position before you took lessons of this man, used to consider to be one and the same that faculty by which white and black are distinguished, which sparrows even see as well as ourselves, and that by which justice and injustice are discriminated, which Tobit also perceived even after he lost the sight of his eyes. If you held the identity, then, of course, when you heard or read the words, "Lighten my eyes, that I sleep not in death," you merely thought of the eyes of the body. Or if this were an obscure point, at all events when you recalled the words of the apostle, "The eyes of your heart being enlightened," you must have supposed that we possessed a heart somewhere between our forehead and cheeks. Well, I am very far from thinking this of you, so that this instructor of yours could not have given you such a lesson.

Chapter 4. —To Believe the Soul is a Part of God is Blasphemy.

And if you happened to suppose, before receiving the instruction from this teacher, which you are rejoicing to have received, that the human soul is a portion of God's nature, then you were ignorant how false and terribly dangerous this opinion was. And if you only were taught by this person that the soul is not a portion of God, then I bid you thank God as earnestly as you can that you were not taken away out of the body before learning so important a lesson. For you would have quitted life a great heretic and a terrible blasphemer. However, I never could have believed this of you, that a man who is both a catholic and a presbyter of no contemptible position like yourself, could by any means have thought that the soul's nature is a portion of God. I therefore cannot help expressing to your beloved self my fears that this man has by some means or other taught you that which is decidedly opposed to the faith which you were holding.

Chapter 5 [III.]—In What Sense Created Beings are Out of God.

Now, just because I do not suppose that you, a member of the catholic Church, ever believed the human soul to be a portion of God, or that the soul's nature is in any degree identical with God's, I have some apprehension lest you may have been induced to fall in with this man's opinion, that "God did not make the soul from nothing, but that the soul is so far out of Him as to have emanated from Him." For he has put out such a statement as this, with his other opinions, which have led him out of the usual track on this subject to a huge precipice. Now, if he has taught you this, I do not want you to teach it to me; nay, I should wish you to unlearn what you have been taught. For it is not enough to avoid believing and saying that the soul is a part of God. We do not even say that the Son or the Holy Ghost is a part of God, although we affirm that the Father, the Son, and the Holy Spirit are all of one and the same nature. It is not, then, enough for us to avoid saying that the soul is a part of God, but it is of indispensable importance that we should say that the soul and God are not of one and the self-same nature. This person is therefore right in declaring that "souls are God's offspring, not by nature, but by gift;" and then, of course, not the souls of all men, but of the faithful. But afterwards he returned to the statement from which he had shrunk, and affirmed that God and the soul are of the same nature—not, indeed, in so many words, but plainly and manifestly to such a purport. For when he says that the soul is out of God, in such a manner that God created it not out of any other nature, nor out of nothing, but out of His own self, what would he have us believe but the very thing which he denies, in other words, even that the soul is of the self-same nature as God Himself is? For every nature is either God, who has no author; or out of God, as having Him for its Author. But the nature which has for its author God, out of whom it comes, is either not made, or made. Now, that nature which is not made and yet is out of Him, is either begotten by Him or proceeds from Him. That which is begotten is His only Son, that which proceeded is the Holy Ghost, and this Trinity is of one and the self-same nature. For these three are one, and each one is God, and all three together are one God, unchangeable, eternal, without any beginning or ending of time. That nature, on the other hand, which is made is called "creature;" God is its Creator, even the blessed Trinity. The creature, therefore, is said to be out of God in such wise as not to be made out of His nature. It is predicated as out of Him, inasmuch as it has in Him the author of its being, not so as to have been born of Him, or to have proceeded from Him, but as having been created, molded, and formed by Him, in some cases, out of no other substance,—that is, absolutely out of nothing, as, for instance, the heaven and the earth, or rather the whole material of the universe coeval in its creation with the world—but, in some cases, out of another nature already created and in existence, as, for instance, man out of the dust, woman out of the man, and man out of his parents. Still, every creature is out of God, —but out of God as its creator either out of nothing, or out of something previously existing, not, however, as its begetter or its producer from His own very self.

Chapter 6. —Shall God's Nature Be Mutable, Sinful, Impious, Even Eternally Damned.

All this, however, I am saying to a catholic: advising with him rather than teaching him. For I do not suppose that these things are new to you; or that they have been long heard of by you, but not believed. This epistle of mine, you will, I am sure, so read as to recognize in its statement your own faith also, which is by the gracious gift of the Lord the common property of us all in the catholic Church. Since, then (as I was saying), I am now speaking to a catholic, whence I pray you tell me, do you suppose that the soul, I will not say your soul or my own soul, but the soul of the first man, was given to him? If you admit that it came from nothing, made, however, and inbreathed into him by God, then your belief tallies with my own. If, on the contrary, you suppose that it came out of some other created thing, which served as the material, as it were, for the divine Artificer to make the soul out of, just as the dust was the material of which Adam was formed, or the rib whence Eve was made, or the waters whence the fishes and the fowls were created, or the ground out of which the terrestrial animals were formed: then this opinion is not catholic, nor is it true. But further, if you think, which may God forbid, that the divine Creator made, or is still making, human souls neither out of nothing, nor out of some other created thing, but out of His own self, that is, out of His own nature, then you have learnt this of your new instructor; but I cannot congratulate you, or flatter you, on the discovery. You have wandered along with him very far from the catholic faith. Better would it be, though it would be untrue, yet it would be better, I say, and more tolerable, that you should believe the soul to have been made out of some other created substance which God had already formed, than out of God's own uncreated substance, so that what is mutable, and sinful, and impious, and if persistent to the end in the impiety will have to suffer eternal damnation, should not with horrible blasphemy be referred to the nature of God! Away, brother, I beseech you, away with this, I will not call it faith, but execrably impious error. May God avert from you, a man of gravity and a presbyter, the misery of being seduced by a youthful layman; and, while supposing that your opinion is the catholic faith, of being lost from the number of the faithful. For I must not deal with you as I might with him; nor does this tremendous error, when yours, deserve the same indulgence as being that of this young man, although you may have derived it from him. He has but just now found his way to the catholic fold to get healing and safety; you have a rank among the very shepherds of that fold. But we would not that a sheep which comes to the Lord's flock for shelter from error, should be healed of his sores in such a way, as first to infect and destroy the shepherd by his contagious presence.

Chapter 7. —To Think the Soul Corporeal an Error.

But if you say to me, He has not taught me this; nor have I by any means given my assent to this erroneous opinion of his, however much I was enchanted by the sweetness of his eloquent and elegant discourse; then I earnestly thank God. Still I cannot help asking, why, even with kisses, as the report goes, you expressed your gratitude to him for having taught you what you were ignorant of, previous to hearing his discussion. Now if it be a false report which makes you to have done and said so much, then I beg you to be kind enough to give me this assurance, that the idle rumor may be stopped by your own written authority. If, however, it is true that you bestowed your thanks with such humility upon this man, I should rejoice, indeed, if he has not taught you to believe the opinion which I have already pointed out as a detestable one, and to be carefully avoided as such. Nor shall I find fault [IV.] if your humble thanks to your instructor were further earned by your having acquired from discussions with him some other true and useful knowledge. But may I ask you what it is? Is it that the soul is not spirit, but body? Well, I really do not think ignorance on such a point is any great injury to Christian learning; and if you indulge in more subtle disputes about the different kinds of bodily substance, I think the information you obtain is more difficult than serviceable. If, however, the Lord will that I should write to this young man himself, as I desire to do, then perhaps your loving self will know to what extent you are not indebted to him for your instruction; although you rejoice in what you have learnt from him. And now I request you not to feel annoyance in writing me an answer; so that what is clearly useful and pertinent to our indispensable faith may not by any chance turn out to be something different.

Chapter 8. —The Thirst of the Rich Man in Hell Does Not Prove the Soul to Be Corporeal.

Now about the point, which with perfect propriety and great soundness of view he believes, that souls after quitting the body are judged, before they come to that final judgment to which they must submit when their bodies are restored to them, and are either tormented or glorified in the very same flesh wherein they once lived here on earth; is it, let me ask you, the case that you were really ignorant of this? Whoever had his mind so obstinately set against the gospel as not to hear these truths, and after hearing to believe them, in the parable of the poor man who was carried away after death to Abraham's bosom, and of the rich man who is set forth as suffering torment in hell? But has this man taught you how it was that the soul apart from the body could crave from the beggar's finger a drop of water; when he himself confessed, that the soul did not require bodily aliment except for the purpose of protecting the perishing body which encloses it from dissolution? These are his words: "Is it," asks he, "because the soul craves meat and drink, that we suppose material food passes into it?" Then shortly afterwards he says: "From this circumstance it is understood and proved, that the sustenance of meat and drink is not wanted for the soul, but for the body: for which clothing also, in addition to food, is provided in like manner; so that the supplying of food seems to be necessary to that nature, which is also fitted for wearing clothes." This opinion of his he expounds clearly enough; but he adds some illustrative similes, and says: "Now what do we suppose the occupier of a house does on an inspection of his dwelling? If he observes the tenement has a shaky roof, or a nodding wall, or a weak foundation, does he not fetch girders and build up buttresses, in order that he may succeed in propping up by his care and diligence the fabric which threatened to fall, so that in the dangerous plight of the residence the peril which evidently overhung the occupier might be warded off?

From this simile," says he, "see how the soul craves for its flesh, from which it undoubtedly conceives the craving itself." Such are the very lucid and adequate words in which this young person has explained his ideas: he asserts that it is not the soul, but the body, which requires food; out of a careful regard, no doubt, of the former for the latter, as one that occupies a dwelling-house, and by a prudent repair prevents the downfall with which the fleshly tenement was threatened. Well, now, let him go on to explain to you what probable ruin this particular soul of the rich man was so eager to prevent by propping up, seeing that it no longer possessed a mortal body, and yet suffered thirst, and begged for the drop of water from the poor man's finger. Here is a good knotty question for this astute instructor of elderly men to exercise himself on; let him inquire, and find a solution if he can: for what purpose did that soul in hell beg the aliment of ever so small a drop of water, when it had no ruinous tenement to support?

Chapter 9 [V.]—How Could the Incorporeal God Breathe Out of Himself a Corporeal Substance?

In that he believes God to be truly incorporeal, I congratulate him that herein, at all events, he has kept himself uninfluenced by the ravings of Tertullian. For he insisted, that as the soul is corporeal, so likewise is God. It is therefore specially surprising that our author, who differs from Tertullian in this point, yet labors to persuade us that the incorporeal God does not make the soul out of nothing, but exhales it as a corporeal breath out of Himself. What a wonderful learning that must be to which every age erects its attentive ears, and which contrives to gain for its disciples men of advanced years, and even presbyters! Let this eminent man read what he has written, read it in public; let him invite to hear the reading well-known persons and unknown ones, learned and unlearned. Old men, assemble with your younger instructors; learn what you used to know nothing about; hear now what you had never heard before. Behold, according to the teaching of this scribe, God creates a breath, not out of something else which exists in some way or other, and not out of that which absolutely has no existence; but out of that which He is Himself, perfectly incorporeal, He breathes a body so that He actually changes His own incorporeal nature into a body, before it undergoes the change into the body of sin. Does he say, that He does not change something out of His own nature, when He creates breath? Then, of course, He does not make that breath out of Himself: for He is not Himself one thing, and His nature another thing. What is this insane man thinking of? But if he says that God creates breath out of His own nature in such a way as to remain absolutely entire Himself, this is not the question. The question is, whether that which comes not of some previously created substance, nor from nothing, but from Him, is not what He is, that is, of the same nature and essence? Now He remains absolutely entire after the generation of His Son; but because He begat Him of His own nature, He did not beget a something which was different from that which He is Himself. For, putting to one side the circumstance that the Word took on Himself a human nature and became flesh, the Word who is the Son of God is another but not another thing: that is, He is another person but not a different nature. And whence does this come to pass, except from the fact that He is not created out of something else, or out of nothing, but was begotten out of Himself; not that He might be better than He was, but that He might be altogether even what He is of whom He is begotten; that is, of one and the same nature, equal, co-eternal, in every way like, equally unchangeable, equally invisible, equally incorporeal, equally God; in a word, that He might be altogether what the Father is, except that He actually is Himself the Son, and not the Father? But if He remains Himself the same God entire and unimpaired, but yet creates something different from Himself, and worse than Himself, not out of nothing, nor out of some other creature, but out of His very self; and that something emanates as a body out of the incorporeal God; then God forbid that a catholic should imbibe such an opinion, for it does not flow from the divine fountain, but it is a mere fiction of the human mind.

Chapter 10 [VI.]—Children May Be Found of Like or of Unlike Dispositions with Their Parents.

Then, again, how ineptly he labors to free the soul, which he supposes to be corporeal, from the passions of the body, raising questions about the soul's infancy; about the soul's emotions, when paralyzed and oppressed; about the amputation of bodily limbs, without cutting or dividing the soul. But in dealing with such points as these, my duty is to treat rather with him than with you; it is for him to labor to assign a reason for all he says. In this way we shall not seem to wish to be too importunate with an elderly man's gravity about a young man's work. As to the similarity of disposition to the parents which is discovered in their children, he does not dispute its coming from the soul's seed. Accordingly, this is the opinion also of those persons who do away with the soul's propagation; but the opposite party who entertain this theory do not place on this the weight of their assertion. For they observe also that children are unlike their parents in disposition; and the reason of this, as they suppose, is, that one and the same person very often has various dispositions himself, unlike each other, —not, of course, that he has received another soul, but that his life has undergone a change for the better or for the worse. So, they say that there is no impossibility in a soul's not possessing the same disposition which he had by whom it was propagated, seeing that the selfsame soul may have different dispositions at different times. If, therefore, you think that you have learnt this of him, that the soul does not come to us by natural transmission at birth, —I only wish that you had discovered from him the truth of the case, —I would with the greatest pleasure resign myself to your hands to learn the whole truth. But really to learn is one thing, and to seem to yourself to have learned is another thing. If, then, you suppose that you have learned what you still are ignorant of, you have evidently not learnt, but given a random credence to a pleasant hearsay. Falsity has stolen over you in the suavity. Now I do not say this from feeling as yet any certainty as to the proposition being false, which asserts that souls are created afresh by God's inbreathing rather than derived from the parents at birth; for I think that this is a point which still requires proof from those who find themselves able to teach it. No; my reason for saying it is, that this person has discussed the whole subject in such a way as not only not to solve the point still in dispute, but even to indulge in statements which leave no doubt as to their falsity. In his desire to prove things of doubtful import, he has boldly stated things which undoubtedly merit reprobation.

Chapter 11 [VII.]—Victor Implies that the Soul Had a "State" And "Merit" Before Incarnation.

Would you hesitate yourself to reprobate what he has said concerning the soul? "You will not have it," he says, "that the soul contracts from the sinful flesh the health, to which holy state you can see it in due course pass by means of the flesh, so as to amend its state through that by which it had lost its merit? Or is it because baptism washes the body that what is believed to be conferred by baptism does not pass on to the soul or spirit? It is only right, therefore, that the soul should, by means of the flesh, repair that old condition which it had seemed to have gradually lost through the flesh, in order that it may begin a regenerate state by means of that whereby it had deserved to be polluted." Now, do observe how grave an error this teacher has fallen into! He says that "the soul repairs its condition by means of the flesh through which it had lost its merit." The soul, then, must have possessed some state and some good merit before the flesh, which he would have that it recovers through the flesh, when the flesh is cleansed in the laver of regeneration. Therefore, before the flesh, the soul had lived somewhere in a good state and merit, which state and merit it lost when it came into the flesh. His words are, "that the soul repairs by means of the flesh that primitive condition which it had seemed to have gradually lost through the flesh." The soul, then, possessed before the flesh, an ancient condition (for his term "primitive" describes the antiquity of the state); and what could that ancient condition have possibly been, but a blessed and laudable state? Now, he avers that this happiness is recovered through the sacrament of baptism, although he will not admit that the soul derives its origin through propagation from that soul which was once manifestly happy in paradise. How is it, then, that in another passage he says that "he constantly affirms of the soul that it exists not by propagation, nor comes out of nothing, nor exists by its own self, nor before the body"? You see how in this place he insists that souls do exist prior to the body somewhere or other, and that in so happy a state that the same happiness is restored to them by means of baptism. But, as if forgetful of his own views, he goes on to speak of its "beginning a regenerate state by means of that," meaning the flesh, "whereby it had deserved to be polluted." In a previous statement he had indicated some good desert which had been lost by means of the flesh; now, however, he speaks of some evil desert, by means of which it had happened that the soul had to come, or be sent, into the flesh; for his words are, "By which it had deserved to be polluted;" and if it deserved to be polluted, its merits could not, of course, have been good. Pray let him tell us what sin it had committed before its pollution by the flesh, in consequence of which it merited such pollution by the flesh. Let him, if he can, explain to us a matter which is utterly beyond his power, because it is certainly far above his reach to discover what to tell us on this subject which shall be true.

Chapter 12 [VIII.]—How Did the Soul Deserve to Be Incarnated?

He also says some time afterwards: "The soul therefore, if it deserved to be sinful, although it could not have been sinful, yet did not remain in sin; because, as it was prefigured in Christ, it was bound not to be in a sinful state, even as it was unable to be." Now, my brother, do you, I ask, really think thus? At any rate, have you formed such an opinion, after having read and duly considered his words, and after having reflected upon what extorted from you praise during his reading, and the expression of your gratitude after he had ended? I pray you, tell me what this means: "Although the soul deserved to be sinful, which could not have been sinful." What mean his phrases, deserved and could not? For it could not possibly have deserved its alleged fate, unless it had been sinful; nor would it have been, unless it could have been, sinful, —so as, by committing sin before any evil desert, it might make for itself a position whence it might, under God's desertion, advance to the commission of other sins. When he said, "which could not have been sinful," did he mean, which would not have been able to be sinful, unless it came in the flesh? But how did it deserve a mission at all into a state where it could be sinful, when it could not possibly have become capable of sinning anywhere else, unless it entered that particular state? Let him, then, tell us how it so deserved. For if it deserved to become capable of sinning, it must certainly have already committed some sin, in consequence of which it deserved to be sinful again. These points, however, may perhaps appear to be obscure, or may be tauntingly said to be of such a character, but they are really most plain and clear. The truth is, he ought not to have said that "the soul deserved to become sinful through the flesh," when he will never be able to discover any desert of the soul, either good or bad, before its being in the flesh.

Chapter 13 [IX.]—Victor Teaches that God Thwarts His Own Predestination.

Let us now go on to plainer matters. For while he was confined within these great straits, as to how souls can be held bound by the chain of original sin, when they derive not their origin from the soul which first sinned, but the Creator breathes them afresh at every birth into sinful flesh,—pure from all contagion and propagation of sin:—in order that he might avoid the objection being brought against his argument, that thus God makes them guilty by such insufflation, he first of all had recourse to the theory drawn from God's prescience, that "He had provided redemption for them." Infants are by the sacrament of this redemption baptized, so that the original sin which they contracted from the flesh is washed away, as if God were remedying His own acts for having made these souls polluted. But afterwards, when he comes to speak of those who receive no such assistance, but expire before they are baptized, he says: "In this place I do not offer myself as an authority, but I present you with an example by way of conjecture. We say, then, that some such method as this must be had recourse to in the case of infants, who, being predestinated for baptism, are yet, by the failing of this life, hurried away before they are born again in Christ. We read," adds he, "it written of such, Speedily was he taken away, lest that wickedness should alter his understanding, or deceit beguile his soul.

Therefore, He hasted to take him away from among the wicked, for his soul pleased the Lord; and, being made perfect in a short time, he fulfilled a long time." Now who would disdain having such a teacher as this? Is it the case, then, with infants, whom people usually wish to have baptized, even hurriedly, before they die, that, if they should be detained ever so short a time in this life, that they might be baptized, and then at once die, wickedness would alter their understanding, and deceit beguile their soul; and to prevent this happening to them, a hasty death came to their rescue, so that they were suddenly taken away before they were baptized? By their very baptism, then, they were changed for the worse, and beguiled by deceit, if it was after baptism that they were snatched away. O excellent teaching, worthy to be admired and closely followed! But he presumed greatly on the prudence of all you who were present at his reading, and especially on yours, to whom he addressed this treatise and handed it after the reading, in supposing that you would believe that the scripture he quoted was intended for the case of unbaptized infants, although it was written of the immature ages of all those saints whom foolish men deem to be hardly dealt with, whenever they are suddenly removed from the present life and are not permitted to attain to the years which people covet for themselves as a great gift of God. What, however, is the meaning of these words of his: "Infants predestinated for baptism, who are yet, by the failing of this life, hurried away before they are born again in Christ," as if some power of fortune, or fate, or anything else you please, did not permit God to fulfil what He had fore-ordained? And how is it that He hurries them Himself away, when they have pleased Him? Then, does He really predestinate them to be baptized, and then Himself hinder the accomplishment of the very thing which He has predestinated?

Chapter 14 [X.]—Victor Sends Those Infants Who Die Unbaptized to Paradise and the Heavenly Mansions, But Not to the Kingdom of Heaven.

But I beg you mark how bold he is, who is displeased with hesitancy, which prefers to be cautious rather than over knowing in a question so profound as this: "I would be bold to say"—such are his words— "that they can attain to the forgiveness of their original sins, yet not so as to be admitted into the kingdom of heaven. Just as in the case of the thief on the cross, who confessed but was not baptized, the Lord did not give him the kingdom of heaven, but paradise; the words remaining accordingly in full force, 'Except a man be born again of water and of the Holy Ghost, he shall not enter into the kingdom of heaven.' This is especially true, since the Lord acknowledges that in His Father's house are many mansions, by which are indicated the many different merits of those who dwell in them; so that in these abodes the unbaptized is brought to forgiveness, and the baptized to the reward which by grace has been prepared for him." You observe how the man keeps paradise and the mansions of the Father's house distinct from the kingdom of heaven, so that even unbaptized persons may have an abundant provision in places of eternal happiness. Nor does he see, when he says all this, that he is so unwilling to distinguish the future abode of a baptized infant from the kingdom of heaven as to have no fear in keeping distinct therefrom the very house of God the Father, or the several parts thereof. For the Lord Jesus did not say: In all the created universe, or in any portion of that universe, but, "In my Father's house, are many mansions." But in what way shall an unbaptized person live in the house of God the Father, when he cannot possibly have God for his Father, except he be born again? He should not be so ungrateful to God, who has vouchsafed to deliver him from the sect of the Donatists or Rogatists, as to aim at dividing the house of God the Father, and to put one portion of it outside the kingdom of heaven, where the unbaptized may be able to dwell. And on what terms does he himself presume that he is to enter into the kingdom of heaven, when from that kingdom he excludes the house of the King Himself, in what part so ever He pleases? From the case, however, of the thief who, when crucified at the Lord's side, put his hope in the Lord who was crucified with him, and from the case of Dinocrates, the brother of St. Perpetua, he argues that even to the unbaptized may be given the remission of sins and an abode with the blessed; as if anyone unbelief in whom would be a sin, had shown him that the thief and Dinocrates had not been baptized. Concerning these cases, however, I have more fully explained my views in the book which I wrote to our brother Renatus. This your loving self will be able to ascertain if you will condescend to read the book; for I am sure our brother will not find it in his heart to refuse you, if you ask him the loan of it.

Chapter 15 [XI.]—Victor "Decides" That Oblations Should Be Offered Up for Those Who Die Unbaptized.

Still he chafes with indecision, and is well-nigh suffocated in the terrible straits of his theory; for very likely he descries with a more sensitive eye than you, the amount of evil which he enunciates, to the effect that original sin in infants is effaced without Christ's sacrament of baptism. It is, indeed, for the purpose of finding an escape to some extent, and tardily, in the Church's sacraments that he says: "In their behalf I most certainly decide that constant oblations and incessant sacrifices must be offered up on the part of the holy priests." Well, then, you may take him if you like for your arbiter, if it were not enough to have him as your instructor. Let him decide that you must offer up the sacrifice of Christ's body even for those who have not been incorporated into Christ. Now this is quite a novel idea, and foreign to the Church's discipline and the rule of truth: and yet, when daring to propound it in his books, he does not modestly say, I rather think; he does not say, I suppose; he does not say, I am of opinion; nor does he say, I at least would suggest, or mention;—but he says, I give it as my decision; so that, should we be (as might be likely) offended by the novelty or the perverseness of his opinion, we might be overawed by the authority of his judicial determination. It is your own concern, my brother, how to be able to bear him as your instructor in these views. Catholic priests, however, of right feeling (and among them you ought to take your place) could never keep quiet—God forbid it—and hear this man pronounce his decisions, when they would wish him rather to recover his senses, and be sorry both for having entertained such opinions, and for having gone so far as to commit them to writing, and chastise himself with the most wholesome discipline of repentance. "Now it is," says he; "on this example of the Maccabees who fell in battle that I ground the necessity of doing this. When they offered stealthily some interdicted sacrifices, and after they had fallen in the battle, we find," says he, "that this remedial measure was at once resorted to by the priests, —sacrifices were offered up to liberate their souls, which had been bound by the guilt of their forbidden conduct." But he says all this, as if (according to his reading of the story) those atoning sacrifices were offered up for uncircumcised persons, as he has decided that these sacrifices of ours must be offered up for unbaptized persons. For circumcision was the sacrament of that period, which prefigured the baptism of our day.

Chapter 16 [XII.]—Victor Promises to the Unbaptized Paradise After Their Death, and the Kingdom of Heaven After Their Resurrection, Although He Admits that This Opposes Christ's Statement.

But your friend, in comparison with what he has shown himself to be further on, thus far makes mistakes which one may somewhat tolerate. He apparently felt some disposition to relent; not, to be sure, at what he ought to have misgivings about, namely, for having ventured to assert that original sin is relaxed even in the case of the unbaptized, and that remission is given to them of all their sins, so that they are admitted into paradise, that is, to a place of great happiness, and possess a claim to the happy mansions in our Father's house; but he seems to have entertained some regret at having conceded to them abodes of lesser blessedness outside the kingdom of heaven. Accordingly he goes on to say, "Or if anyone is perhaps reluctant to believe that paradise is bestowed as a temporary and provisional gift on the soul of the thief or of Dinocrates (for there remains for them still, in the resurrection, the reward of the kingdom of heaven), although that principal passage stands in the way,—'Except a man be born again of water and of the Spirit, he shall not enter into the kingdom of God.'—he may yet hold my assent as ungrudgingly given to this point; only let him magnify both the aim and the effect of the divine compassion and fore-knowledge." These words have I copied, as I read them in his second book. Well, now, could anyone have shown on this erroneous point greater boldness, recklessness, or presumption? He actually quotes and calls attention to the Lord's weighty sentence, encloses it in a statement of his own, and then says, "Although the opinion is opposed to the 'principal passage,' 'Except a man be born again of water and of the Spirit, he shall not enter into the kingdom of God;'" he dares then to lift his haughty head in censure against the Prince's judgment: "He may yet hold my assent as ungrudgingly given to this point;" and he explains his point to be, that the souls of unbaptized persons have a claim to paradise as a temporary gift; and in this class he mentions the dying thief and Dinocrates, as if he were prescribing, or rather prejudging, their destination; moreover, in the resurrection, he will have them transferred to a better provision, even making them receive the reward of the kingdom of heaven. "Although," says he, "this is opposed to the sentence of the Prince." Now, do you, my brother, I pray you, seriously consider this question: What sentence of the Prince shall that man deserve to have passed upon him, who imposes on any person an assent of his own which runs counter to the authority of the Prince Himself?

Chapter 17.—Disobedient Compassion and Compassionate Disobedience Reprobated. Martyrdom in Lieu of Baptism.

The new-fangled Pelagian heretics have been most justly condemned by the authority of catholic councils and of the Apostolic See, on the ground of their having dared to give to unbaptized infants a place of rest and salvation, even apart from the kingdom of heaven. This they would not have dared to do, if they did not deny their having original sin, and the need of its remission by the sacrament of baptism. This man, however, professes the catholic belief on this point, admitting that infants are tied in the bonds of original sin, and yet he releases them from these bonds without the laver of regeneration, and after death, in his compassion, he admits them into paradise; while, with a still ampler compassion, he introduces them after the resurrection even to the kingdom of heaven. Such compassion did Saul see fit to assume when he spared the king whom God commanded to be slain; deservedly, however, was his disobedient compassion, or (if you prefer it) his compassionate disobedience, reprobated and condemned, that man may be on his guard against extending mercy to his fellow-man, in opposition to the sentence of Him by whom man was made. Truth, by the mouth of Itself incarnate, proclaims as if in a voice of thunder: "Except a man be born again of water and of the Spirit, he cannot enter into the kingdom of God." And in order to except martyrs from this sentence, to whose lot it has fallen to be slain for the name of Christ before being washed in the baptism of Christ, He says in another passage, "He that loses his life for my sake shall find it." And so far from promising the abolition of original sin to anyone who has not been regenerated in the laver of Christian faith, the apostle exclaims, "By the offence of one, judgment came upon all men to condemnation." And as a counterbalance against this condemnation, the Lord exhibits the help of His salvation alone, saying, "He that believeth, and is baptized, shall be saved; but he that believeth not shall be damned." Now the mystery of this believing in the case of infants is completely affected by the response of the sureties by whom they are taken to baptism; and unless this be affected, they all pass by the offence of one into condemnation. And yet, in opposition to such clear declarations uttered by the Truth, forth marches before all men a vanity which is more foolish than pitiful, and says: Not only do infants not pass into condemnation, though no laver of Christian faith absolves them from the chain of original sin, but they even after death have an intermediate enjoyment of the felicities of paradise, and after the resurrection they shall possess even the happiness of the kingdom of heaven. Now, would this man dare to say all this in opposition to the firmly-established catholic faith, if he had not presumptuously undertaken to solve a question which transcends his powers touching the origin of the soul?

Chapter 18 [XIII.]—Victor's Dilemma and Fall.

For he is hemmed in within terrible straits by those who make the natural inquiry: "Why has God visited on the soul so unjust a punishment as to have willed to relegate it into a body of sin, since by its consorting with the flesh that began to be sinful, which else could not have been sinful?" For, of course, they say: "The soul could not have been sinful, if God had not commingled it in the participation of sinful flesh." Well, this opponent of mine was unable to discover the justice of God's doing this, especially in consequence of the eternal damnation of infants who die without the remission of original sin by baptism; and his inability was equally great in finding out why the good and righteous God both bound the souls of infants, who He foresaw would derive no advantage from the sacrament of Christian grace, with the chain of original sin, by sending them into the body which they derive from Adam,—the souls themselves being free from all taint of propagation,—and by this means also made them amenable to eternal damnation. No less was he unwilling to admit that these very souls likewise derived their sinful origin from that one primeval soul. And so he preferred escaping by a miserable shipwreck of faith, rather than to furl his sails and steady his oars, in the voyage of his controversy, and by such prudent counsel check the fatal rashness of his course. Worthless in his youthful eye was our aged caution; just as if this most troublesome and perilous question of his was more in need of a torrent of eloquence than the counsel of prudence. And this was foreseen even by himself, but to no purpose; for, as if to set forth the points which were objected to him by his opponents, he says: "After them other reproachful censures are added to the querulous murmurings of those who rail against us; and, as if tossed about in a whirlwind, we are dashed repeatedly among huge rocks." After saying this, he propounded for himself the very dangerous question, which we have already treated, wherein he has wrecked the catholic faith, unless by a real repentance he shall have repaired the faith which he had shattered. That whirlwind and those rocks I have myself avoided, unwilling to entrust my frail barque to their dangers; and when writing on this subject I have expressed myself in such a way as rather to explain the grounds of my hesitancy, than to exhibit the rashness of presumption. This little work of mine excited his derision, when he met with it at your house, and in utter recklessness he flung himself upon the reef: he showed more spirit than wisdom in his conduct. To what lengths, however, that overconfidence of his led him, I suppose that you can now yourself perceive. But I give heartier thanks to God, since you even before this descried it. For all the while he was refusing to check his headlong career, when the issue of his course was still in doubt, he alighted on his miserable enterprise, and maintained that God, in the case of infants who died without Christian regeneration, conferred upon them paradise at once, and ultimately the kingdom of heaven.

Chapter 19 [XIV.]—Victor Relies on Ambiguous Scriptures.

The passages of Scripture, indeed, which he has adduced in the attempt to prove from them that God did not derive human souls by propagation from the primitive soul, but as in that first instance that He formed them by breathing them into each individual, are so uncertain and ambiguous, that they can with the utmost facility be taken in a different sense from that which he would assign to them. This point I have already demonstrated with sufficient clearness, I think in the book which I addressed to that friend of ours, of whom I have made mention above. The passages which he has used for his proofs inform us that God gives, or makes, or fashion men's souls; but whence He gives them, or of what He makes or fashions them, they tell us nothing: they leave untouched the question whether it be by propagation from the first soul or by insufflation, like the first soul. This writer however, simply because he reads that God "giveth" souls, "hath made" souls, "formed" souls, supposes that these phrases amount to a denial of the propagation of souls; whereas, by the testimony of the same scripture, God gives men their bodies, or makes them, or fashions and forms them; although no one doubts that the said bodies are given, made, and formed by Him by seminal propagation.

Chapter 20. —Victor Quotes Scriptures for Their Silence, and Neglects the Biblical Usage.

As for the passage which affirms that "God hath made of one blood all nations of men," and that in which Adam says, "This is now bone of my bones, and flesh of my flesh," inasmuch as it is not said in the one, "of one soul," and in the other, "soul of my soul," he supposes that it is denied that children's souls come from their parents, or the first woman's from her husband just as if, forsooth, had the sentence run in the way suggested, "of one soul," instead of "of one blood," anything else than the whole human being could be understood, without any denial of the propagation of the body. So likewise, if it had been said, "soul of my soul," the flesh would not be denied, of course, which evidently had been taken out of the man. Constantly does Holy Scripture indicate the whole by a part, and a part by the whole. For certainly, if in the passage which this man has quoted as his proof it had been said that the human race had been made, not "of one blood," but "of one man," it could not have prejudiced the opinion of those who deny the propagation of souls, although man is not soul alone, nor only flesh, but both. For they would have their answer ready to this effect, that the Scripture here might have meant to indicate a part by the whole, that is to say, the flesh only by the entire human being. In like manner, they who maintain the propagation of souls contend that in the passage where it is said, "of one blood," the human being is implied by the term "blood," on the principle of the whole being expressed by a part. For just as the one party seems to be assisted by the expression, "of one blood," instead of the phrase, "of one man," so the other side evidently gets countenance from the statement being so plainly written, "By one man sin entered into the world, and death by sin; and so death passed upon all men, for in him all sinned," instead of its being said, "in whom the flesh of all sinned." Similarly, as one party seems to receive assistance from the fact that Scripture says, "This is now bone of my bones, and flesh of my flesh," on the ground that a part covers the whole; so, again, the other side derives some advantage from what is written in the immediate sequel of the passage, "She shall be called woman, because she was taken out of her husband." For, according to their contention, the latter clause should have run, "Because her flesh was taken out of her husband," if it was not true that the entire woman, soul and all, but only her flesh, was taken out of man. The fact, however, of the whole matter is simply this, that after hearing both sides, anybody whose judgment is free from party prejudice sees at once that loose quotation is unavailing in this controversy; for against one party, which maintains the opinion of the propagation of souls, those passages must not be adduced which mention only a part, inasmuch as the Scripture might mean by the part to imply the whole in all such passages; as, for instance, when we read, "The Word was made flesh," we of course understand not the flesh only, but the entire human being; nor against the other party, who deny this doctrine of the soul's propagation, is it of any avail to quote those passages which do not mention a part of the human being, but the whole; because in these the Scripture might possibly mean to imply a part by the whole; as we confess that Christ was buried, whereas it was only His flesh that was laid in the sepulcher. We therefore say, that on such grounds there is no ground on the one hand for rashly constructing, nor on the other hand for, with equal rashness, demolishing the theory of propagation; but we add this advice, that other passages be duly looked out, such as admit of no ambiguity.

Chapter 21 [XV.]—Victor's Perplexity and Failure.

For these reasons I fail thus far to discover what this instructor has taught you, and what grounds you have for the gratitude you have lavished upon him. For the question remains just as it was, which inquiries about the origin of souls, whether God gives, forms, and makes them for men by propagating them from that one soul which He breathed into the first man, or whether it is by His own inbreathing that He does this in every case, as He did for the first man. For that God does form, and make, and bestow souls on men, the Christian faith does not hesitate to aver. Now, when this person endeavored to solve the question without gauging his own resources, by denying the propagation of souls, and asserting that the Creator inbreathed them into men pure from all contagion of sin, —not out of nothing, but out of Himself, —He dishonored the very nature of God by opprobriously attributing mutability to it, an imputation which was necessarily untenable. Then, desirous of avoiding all implication which might lead to God's being deemed unrighteous, if He ties with the bond of original sin souls which are pure of all actual sin, although not redeemed by Christian regeneration, he has given utterance to words and sentiments which I only wish he had not taught you. For he has accorded to unbaptized infants such happiness and salvation as even the Pelagian heresy could not have ventured on doing. And yet for all this, when the question touches the many thousands of infants who are born of the ungodly, and die among the ungodly,—I do not mean those whom charitable persons are unable to assist by baptism, however desirous of doing so, but those of whose baptism nobody either has been able or shall be able to think, and for whom no one has offered or is likely to offer the sacrifice which, as this instructor of yours thought, ought to be offered even for those who have not been baptized,—he has discovered no means of solving it. If he were questioned concerning them, what their souls deserved that God should involve them in sinful flesh to incur eternal damnation, never to be washed in the laver of baptism, nor atoned for by the sacrifice of Christ's body and blood, he will then either feel himself at an utter loss, and so will regard our hesitation with a real, though tardy favor; or else will determine that Christ's body must be offered for all those infants which all the world over die without Christian baptism (their names having been never heard of, since they are unknown in the Church of Christ), although not incorporated into the body of Christ.

Chapter 22 [XVI.]—Peter's Responsibility in the Case of Victor.

Far be it from you, my brother, that such views should be pleasant to you, or that you should either feel pleasure in having acquired them, or presume ever to teach them. Otherwise, even he would be a far better man than yourself. Because at the commencement of his first book he has prefixed the following modest and humble preface: "Though I desire to comply with your request, I am only affording a clear proof of my presumption." And a little further on he says, "Inasmuch as I am, indeed, by no means confident of being able to prove what I may have advanced; and moreover I should always be anxious not to insist on any opinion of my own, if it is found to be an improbable one; and it would be my hearty desire, in case my own judgment is condemned, earnestly to follow better and truer views. For as it shows evidence of the best intention, and a laudable purpose, to permit yourself to be easily led to truer views of a subject; so it betokens an obstinate and depraved mind to refuse to turn quickly aside into the pathway of reason." Now, as he said all this sincerely, and still feels as he spoke, he no doubt entertains a very hopeful feeling about a right issue. In similar strain he concludes his second book: "You must not think," says he, "that there is any chance of its ever recoiling invidiously against you, that I constitute you the judge of my words. And lest by chance the sharp eye of some inquisitive reader may have opportunity of turning up and encountering any possible vestiges of elemental error which may be left behind on my illegal sheets, I beg you to tear up page after page with unsparing hand, if need be; and after expending on me your critical censure, punish me further, by smearing out the very ink which has given form to my worthless words; so that, having your full opportunity, you may prevent all ridicule, on the score either of the favorable opinion you so strongly entertain of me, or of the inaccuracies which lurk in my writings."

Chapter 23 [XVII.]—Who They are that are Not Injured by Reading Injurious Books.

Forasmuch, then, as he has both commenced and terminated his books with such safeguards, and has placed on your shoulders the religious burden of their correction and emendation, I only trust that he may find in you all that he has asked you for, that you may "correct him righteously in mercy, and reprove him; whilst the oil of the sinner which anoints his head" is absent from your hands and eyes, —even the indecent compliance of the flatterer, and the deceitful leniency of the sycophant. If, however, you decline to apply correction when you see anything to amend, you offend against love; but if he does not appear to you to require correction, because you think him to be right in his opinions, then you are wise against truth. He, therefore, is a better man (since he is only too ready to be corrected, if a true censurer be at hand) than yourself, if either knowing him to be in error you despise him with derision, or ignorant of his wandering course you at the same time closely follow his error. Everything, therefore, which you find in the books that he has addressed and forwarded to you, I beg you to consider with sobriety and vigilance; and you will perhaps make fuller discoveries than I have myself of statements which deserve to be censured. And as for such of their contents as are worthy of praise and approbation,—whatever good you have learnt therein, and by his instruction, which perhaps you were really ignorant of before, tell us plainly what it is, that all may know that it was for this particular benefit that you expressed your obligations to him, and not for the manifold statements in his books which call for their disapproval,—all, I mean, who, like yourself, heard him read his writings, or who afterwards read the same for themselves: lest in his ornate style they may drink poison, as out of a choice goblet, at your instance, though not after your own example, because they know not precisely what it is you have drunk yourself, and what you have left untasted, and because, from your high character, they suppose that whatever is drunk out of this fountain would be for their health. For what else are hearing, and reading, and copiously depositing things in the memory, than several processes of drinking? The Lord, however, foretold concerning His faithful followers, that even "if they should drink any deadly thing, it should not hurt them." And thus it happens that they who read with judgment, and bestow their approbation on whatever is commendable according to the rule of faith, and disapprove of things which ought to be reprobated, even if they commit to their memory statements which are declared to be worthy of disapproval, they receive no harm from the poisonous and depraved nature of the sentences. To myself, through the Lord's mercy, it can never become a matter of the least regret, that, actuated by our previous love, I have given your reverend and religious self-advice and warning on these points, in whatever way you may receive the admonition for which I have regarded you as possessing the first claim upon me. Abundant thanks, indeed, shall I give unto Him in whose mercy it is most salutary to put one's trust, if this letter of mine shall either find or else make your faith both free from the depraved and erroneous opinions which I have been able herein to point out from this man's books, and sound in catholic integrity.

Book III.

ADDRESSED TO VINCENTIUS VICTOR.

Augustin points out to Vincentius Victor the corrections which he ought to make in his books concerning the origin of the soul, if he wishes to be a Catholic. Those opinions also which had been already refuted in the preceding books addressed to Renatus and Peter, Augustin briefly censures in this third book, which is written to Victor himself: moreover, he classifies them under eleven heads of error.

Chapter 1 [I.]—Augustin's Purpose in Writing.

As to that which I have thought it my duty to write to you, my much-loved son Victor, I would have you to entertain this above all other thoughts in your mind, if I seemed to despise you, that it was certainly not my intention to do so. At the same time, I must beg of you not to abuse our condescension in such a way as to suppose that you possess my approval merely because you have not my contempt. For it is not to follow, but to correct you, that I give you my love; and since I by no means despair of the possibility of your amendment, I do not want you to be surprised at my inability to despise the man who has my love. Now, since it was my bounden duty to love you before you had united with us, in order that you might become a catholic; how much more ought I now to love you since your union with us, to prevent your becoming a new heretic, and that you may become so firm a catholic that no heretic may be able to withstand you! So far as appears from the mental endowments which God has largely bestowed upon you, you would be undoubtedly a wise man if you only did not believe that you were one already, and begged of Him who makes men wise, with a pious, humble, and earnest prayer, that you might become one, and preferred not to be led astray with error rather than to be honored with the flattery of those who go astray.

Chapter 2 [II.]—Why Victor Assumed the Name of Vincentius. The Names of Evil Men Ought Never to Be Assumed by Other Persons.

The first thing which caused me some anxiety about you was the title which appeared in your books with your name; for on inquiring of those who knew you, and were probably your associates in opinion, who Vincentius Victor was, I found that you had been a Donatist, or rather a Rogatist, but had lately come into communion with the catholic Church. Now, while I was rejoicing, as one naturally does at the recovery of those whom he sees rescued from that system of error,—and in your case my joy was all the greater because I saw that your ability, which so much delighted me in your writings, had not remained behind with the enemies of truth,—additional information was given me by your friends which caused me sorrow amid my joy, to the effect that you wished to have the name Vincentius prefixed to your own name, inasmuch as you still held in affectionate regard the successor of Rogatus, who bore this name, as a great and holy man, and that for this reason you wished his name to become your surname. Some persons also told me that you had, moreover, boasted about his having appeared in some sort of a vision to you, and assisted you in composing those books the subject of which I have discussed with you in this small work of mine, and to such an extent as to dictate to you himself the precise topics and arguments which you were to write about. Now, if all this be true, I no longer wonder at your having been able to make those statements which, if you will only lend a patient ear to my admonition, and with the attention of a catholic duly consider and weigh those books, you will undoubtedly come to regret having ever advanced. For he who, according to the apostle's portrait, "transforms himself into an angel of light," has transformed himself before you into a shape which you believe to have been, or still to be, an angel of light. In this way, indeed, he is less able to deceive Catholics when his transformations are not into angels of light, but into heretics; now, however, that you are a catholic, I should be sorry for you to be beguiled by him. He will certainly feel torture at your having learnt the truth, and so much the more in proportion to the pleasure he formerly experienced in having persuaded you to believe error. With a view, however, to your refraining from loving a dead person, when the love can neither be serviceable to yourself nor profitable to him, I advise you to consider for a moment this one point—that he is not, of course, a just and holy man, since you withdrew yourself from the snares of the Donatists or Rogatists on the score of their heresy; but if you do think him to be just and holy, you ruin yourself by holding communion with Catholics. You are, indeed, only feigning yourself a catholic if you are in mind the same as he was on whom you bestow your love; and you are aware how terribly the Scripture has spoken on this subject: "The Holy Spirit of discipline will flee from the man who feigns." If, however, you are sincere in communicating with us, and do not merely pretend to be a catholic, how is it that you still love a dead man to such a degree as to be willing even now to boast of the name of one in whose errors you no longer permit yourself to be held? We really do not like your having such a surname, as if you were the monument of a dead heretic. Nor do we like your book to have such a title as we should say was a false one if we read it on his tomb. For we are sure Vincentius is not Victor, the conqueror, but Victus, the conquered; —may it be, however, with fruitful effect, even as we wish you to be conquered by the truth! And yet your thought was an astute and skillful one, when you designated the books, which you wish us to suppose were dictated to you by his inspiration, by the name of Vincentius Victor; as much as to intimate that it was rather he than you who wished to be designated by the victorious appellation, as having been himself the conqueror of error, by revealing to you what were to be the contents of your written treatise. But of what avail is all this to you, my son? Be, I pray you, a true catholic, not a feigned one, lest the Holy Spirit should flee from you, and that Vincentius be unable to profit you at all, into whom the most malignant spirit of error has transformed himself for the purpose of deceiving you; for it is from that one that all these evil opinions have proceeded, notwithstanding the artful fraud which has persuaded you to the contrary. If this admonition shall only induce you to correct these errors with the humility of a God-fearing man and the peaceful submission of a catholic, they will be regarded as the mistakes of an over-zealous young man, who is eager rather to amend them than to persevere in them. But if he shall have by his influence prevailed on you to contend for these opinions with obstinate perseverance, which God forbid, it will in such a case be necessary to condemn them and their author as heretical, as is required by the pastoral and remedial nature of the Church's charge, to check the dire contagion before it quietly spreads through the heedless masses, while wholesome correction is neglected, under the name but without the reality of love.

Chapter 3 [III.]—He Enumerates the Errors Which He Desires to Have Amended in the Books of Vincentius Victor. The First Error.

If you ask me what the particular errors are, you may read what I have written to our brethren, that servant of God Renatus, and the presbyter Peter, to the latter of whom you yourself thought it necessary to write the very works of which we are now treating, "in obedience," as you allege, "to his own wish and request." Now, they will, I doubt not, lend you my treatises for your perusal if you should like it, and even press them upon your attention without being asked. But be that as it may, I will not miss this present opportunity of informing you what amendments I desire to have made in these writings of yours, as well as in your belief. The first is, that you will have it that "The soul was not so made by God that He made it out of nothing, but out of His own very self." Here you do not reflect what the necessary conclusion is, that the soul must be of the nature of God; and you know very well, of course, how impious such an opinion is. Now, to avoid such impiety as this, you ought so to say that God is the Author of the soul as that it was made by Him, but not of Him. For whatever is of Him (as, for instance, His only-begotten Son) is of the self-same nature as Himself. But, that the soul might not be of the same nature as its Creator, it was made by Him, but not of Him. Or, then, tell me whence it is, or else confess that it is of nothing. What do you mean by that expression of yours, "That it is a certain particle of an exhalation from the nature of God"? Do you mean to say, then, that the exhalation itself from the nature of God, to which the particle in question belongs, is not of the same nature as God is Himself? If this be your meaning, then God made out of nothing that exhalation of which you will have the soul to be a particle. Or, if not out of nothing, pray tell me of what God made it? If He made it out of Himself, it follows that He is Himself (what should never be affirmed) the material of which His own work is formed. But you go on to say: "When however, He made the exhalation or breath out of Himself, He remained at the same time whole and entire;" just as if the light of a candle did not also remain entire when another candle is lighted from it, and yet be of the same nature, and not another.

Chapter 4 [IV.]—Victor's Simile to Show that God Can Create by Breathing Without Impartation of His

Substance.

"But," you say, "when we inflate a bag, no portion of our nature or quality is poured into the bag, while the very breath, by the current of which the filled bag is extended, is emitted from us without the least diminution of ourselves." Now, you enlarge and dwell upon these words of yours, and inculcate the simile as necessary for our understanding how it is that God, without any injury to His own nature, makes the soul out of His own self, and how, when it is thus made out of Himself, it is not what Himself is. For you ask: "Is this inflation of the bag a portion of our own soul? Or do we create human beings when we inflate bags? Or do we suffer any injury in anything at all when we impart our breath by inflation on diverse things? But we suffer no injury when we transfer breath from ourselves to anything, nor do we ever remember experiencing any damage to ourselves from inflating a bag, the full quality and entire quantity of our breath remaining in us notwithstanding the process." Now, however elegant and applicable this simile seems to you, I beg you to consider how greatly it misleads you. For you affirm that the incorporeal God breathes out a corporeal soul, —not made out of nothing, but out of Himself, —whereas the breath which we ourselves emit is corporeal, although of a subtler nature than our bodies; nor do we exhale it out of our soul, but out of the air through internal functions in our bodily structure. Our lungs, like a pair of bellows, are moved by the soul (at the command of which also the other members of the body are moved), for the purpose of inhaling and exhaling the atmospheric air. For, besides the aliments, solid or fluid, which constitute our meat and drink, God has surrounded us with this third aliment of the atmosphere which we breathe; and that with so good effect, that we can live for some time without meat and drink, but we could not possibly subsist for a moment without this third aliment, which the air, surrounding us on all sides, supplies us with as we breathe and respire. And as our meat and drink have to be not only introduced into the body, but also to be expelled by passages formed for the purpose, to prevent injury accruing either way (from either not entering or not quitting the body); so this third airy aliment (not being permitted to remain within us, and thus not becoming corrupt by delay, but being expelled as soon as it is introduced) has been furnished, not with different, but with the self-same channels both for its entrance and for its exit, even the mouth, or the nostrils, or both together.

Chapter 5. —Examination of Victor's Simile: Does Man Give Out Nothing by Breathing?

Prove now yourself what I say, for your own satisfaction in your own case; emit breath by exhalation, and see whether you can continue long without catching back your breath; then again catch it back by inhalation, and see what discomfort you experience unless you again emit it. Now, when we inflate a bag, as you prescribe, we do, in fact, the same thing which we do to maintain life, except that in the case of the artificial experiment our inhalation is somewhat stronger, in order that we may emit a stronger breath, so as to fill and distend the bag by compressing the air we blow into it, rather in the manner of a hard puff than of the gentle process of ordinary breathing and respiration. On what ground, then, do you say, "We suffer no injury whenever we transfer breath from ourselves to any object, nor do we ever remember experiencing any damage to ourselves from inflating a bag, the full quality and entire quantity of our own breath remaining in us notwithstanding the process"? It is very plain, my son, if ever you have inflated a bag, that you did not carefully observe your own performance. For you do not perceive what you lose by the act of inflation because of the immediate recovery of your breath. But you can learn all this with the greatest ease if you would simply prefer doing so to stiffly maintaining your own statements for no other reason than because you have made them—not inflating the bag, but inflated yourself to the full, and inflating your hearers (whom you should rather edify and instruct by veritable facts) with the empty prattle of your turgid discourse. In the present case I do not send you to any other teacher than your own self. Breathe, then, a good breath into the bag; shut your mouth instantly, hold tight your nostrils, and in this way discover the truth of what I say to you. For when you begin to suffer the intolerable inconvenience which accompanies the experiment, what is it you wish to recover by opening your mouth and releasing your nostrils? Surely there would be nothing to recover if your supposition be a correct one, that you have lost nothing whenever you breathe. Observe what a plight you would be in, if by inhalation you did not regain what you had parted with by your breathing outwards. See, too, what loss and injury the insufflation would produce, were it not for the repair and reaction caused by respiration. For unless the breath which you expend in filling the bag should all return by the re-opened channel to discharge its function of nourishing yourself, what, I wonder, would be left remaining to you, —I will not say to inflate another bag, but to supply your very means of living?

Chapter 6. —The Simile Reformed in Accordance with Truth.

Well, now, you ought to have thought of all this when you were writing, and not to have brought God before our eyes in that favorite simile of yours, of inflated and inflatable bags, breathing forth souls out of some other nature which was already in existence, just as we ourselves make our breath from the air which surrounds us; or certainly you should not, in a manner which is really as diverse from your similitude as it is abundant in impiety, have represented God as either producing some changeable thing without injury, indeed, to Himself, but yet out of His own substance; or what is worse, creating it in such wise as to be Himself the material of His own work. If, however, we are to employ a similitude drawn from our breathing which shall suitably illustrate this subject, the following one is more credible: Just as we, whenever we breathe, make a breath, not out of our own nature, but, because we are not omnipotent, out of that air that surrounds us, which we inhale and discharge whenever we breathe and respire; and the said breath is neither living nor sentient, although we are ourselves living and sentient; so God can—not, indeed, out of His own nature, but (as being so omnipotent as to be able to create whatever He wills) even out of that which has no existence at all, that is to say, out of nothing—make a breath that is living and sentient, but evidently mutable, though He be Himself immutable.

Chapter 7 [V.]—Victor Apparently Gives the

St. Augustine

Creative Breath to Man Also.

But what is the meaning of that, which you have thought proper to add to this simile, about the example of the blessed Elisha because he raised the dead by breathing into his face? Now, do you really suppose that Elisha's breath was made the soul of the child? I could not believe that even you could stray so far away from the truth. If, now, that soul which was taken from the living child so as to cause his death, was itself afterwards restored to him so as to cause his restoration to life: where, I ask, is the pertinence of your remark when you say, "that no diminution accrued to Elisha," as if it could be imagined that anything had been transferred from the prophet to the child to cause his revival? But if you meant no more than that the prophet breathed and remained entire, where was the necessity for your saying that of Elisha, when raising the dead child, which you might with no less propriety say of any one whatever when emitting a breath, and reviving no one? Then, again, you spoke unadvisedly (though God forbid that you should believe the breath of Elisha to have become the soul of the resuscitated child!) when you intimated your meaning to be a desire to keep separate what was first done by God from this that was done by the prophet, in that the One breathed but once, and the other thrice. These are your words: "Elisha breathed into the face of the deceased child of the Shunammite, after the manner of the original creation. And when by the prophet's breathing a divine force inspired the dead limbs, reanimated to their original vigor, no diminution accrued to Elisha, through whose breathing the dead body recovered its revived soul and spirit. Only there is this difference, the Lord breathed but once into man's face and he lived, while Elisha breathed three times into the face of the dead and he lived again." Thus, your words sound as if the number of the breathings alone made all the difference, why we should not believe that the prophet actually did what God did. This statement, then, requires to be entirely revised. There was so complete a difference between that work of God and this of Elisha, that the former breathed the breath of life whereby man became a living soul, and the latter breathed a breath which was not itself sentient nor endued with life, but was figurative for the sake of some signification. The prophet did not really cause the child to live again by giving him life, but he procured God's doing that by giving him love. As to what you allege, that he breathed three times, either your memory, as often happens, or a faulty reading of the text, must have misled you. Why need I enlarge? You ought not to be seeking for examples and arguments to establish your point, but rather to amend and change your opinion. I beg of you neither to believe, nor to say, nor to teach "that God made the human soul not out of nothing, but out of His own substance," if you wish to be a catholic.

Chapter 8 [VI.]—Victor's Second Error. (See Above in Book I. 26 [XVI.].)

Do not, I pray you, believe, say, or teach that "Thus is God ever giving souls through infinite time, just as He who gives is Himself ever existent," if you wish to be a catholic. For a time will come when God will not give souls, although He will not therefore Himself cease to exist. Your phrase, "is ever giving," might be understood "to give without cessation," so long as men are born and get offspring, even as it is said of certain men that they are "ever learning, and never coming to the knowledge of the truth." For this term "ever" is not in this passage taken to mean "never ceasing to learn," inasmuch as they do cease to learn when they have ceased to exist in this body, or have begun to suffer the fiery pains of hell. You, however, did not allow your word to be understood in this sense when you said, "is ever giving," since you thought that it must be applied to infinite time. And even this was a small matter; for, as if you had been asked to explain your phrase, "ever giving," more explicitly, you went on to say, "just as He is Himself ever existent who gives." This assertion the sound and catholic faith utterly condemns. For be it far from us to believe that God is ever giving souls, just as He is Himself, who gives them, ever existent. He is Himself ever existent in such a sense as never to cease to exist; souls, however, He will not be ever giving; but He will beyond doubt cease to give them when the age of generation ceases, and children are no longer born to whom they are to be given.

Chapter 9 [VII.]—His Third Error. (See Above in Book II. 11 [VII.].)

Again, do not, I pray you, believe, say, or teach that "the soul deservedly lost something by the flesh, although it was of good merit before the flesh," if you wish to be a catholic. For the apostle declares that "children who are not yet born, have done neither good nor evil." How, therefore, could their soul, before its participation of flesh, have had anything like good desert, if it had not done any good thing? Will you by any chance venture to assert that it had, before the flesh, lived a good life, when you cannot actually prove to us that it even existed at all? How, then, can you say: "You will not allow that the soul contracts health from the sinful flesh; and to this holy state, then, you can see it in due course pass, with the view of amending its condition, through that very flesh by which it had lost merit"? Perhaps you are not aware that these opinions, which attribute to the human soul a good state and a good merit before the flesh, have been already condemned by the catholic Church, not only in the case of some ancient heretics, whom I do not here mention, but also more recently in the instance of the Priscillianists.

Chapter 10. —His Fourth Error. (See Above in Book I. 6 [VI.] and Book II. 11 [VII.].)

Neither believe, nor say, nor teach that "the soul, by means of the flesh, repairs its ancient condition, and is born again by the very means through which it had deserved to be polluted," if you wish to be a catholic. I might, indeed, dwell upon the strange discrepancy with your own self which you have exhibited in the next sentence, wherein you said that the soul through the flesh deservedly recovers its primitive condition, which it had seemed to have gradually lost through the flesh, in order that it may begin to be regenerated by the very flesh through which it had deserved to be polluted." Here you—the very man who had just before said that the soul repairs its condition through the flesh, by reason of which it had lost its desert (where nothing but good desert can be meant, which you will have to be recovered in the flesh, by baptism, of course)—said in another turn of your thought, that through the flesh the soul had deserved to be polluted (in which statement it is no longer the good desert, but an evil one, which must be meant). What flagrant inconsistency! but I will pass it over, and content myself with observing, that it is absolutely uncatholic to believe that the soul, before its incarnate state, deserved either good or evil.

Chapter 11 [VIII.]—His Fifth Error. (See Above in Book I. 8 [VIII.] and Book II. 12 [VIII.].)

Neither believe, nor say, nor teach, if you wish to be a catholic, that "the soul deserved to be sinful before any sin." It is, to be sure, an extremely bad desert to have deserved to be sinful. And, of course, it could not possibly have incurred so bad a desert before any sin, especially prior to its coming into the flesh, when it could have possessed no merit either way, either evil or good. How, then, can you say: "If, therefore, the soul, which could not be sinful, deserved to be sinful, it yet did not remain in sin, because as it was prefigured in Christ it was bound not to be in a sinful state, even as it was unable to be"? Now, just for a little consider what it is you say, and desist from repeating such a statement. How did the soul deserve, and how was it unable, to be sinful? How, I pray you tell me, did that deserve to be sinful which never lived sinfully? How, I ask again, was that made sinful which was not able to be sinful? Or else, if you mean your phrase, "was unable," to imply inability apart from the flesh, how in that case did the soul deserve to be sinful, and because of what desert was it sent into the flesh, when before its union with the flesh it was not able to be sinful, so as to deserve any evil at all?

A Treatise on the Soul and its Origin

Chapter 12 [IX.]—His Sixth Error. (See Above in Book I. 10-12 [IX., X.], and in Book II. 13, 14 [IX., X.].)

If you wish to be a catholic, refrain from believing, or saying, or teaching that "infants which are forestalled by death before they are baptized may yet attain to forgiveness of their original sins." For the examples by which you are misled—that of the thief who confessed the Lord upon the cross, or that of Dinocrates the brother of St. Perpetua—contribute no help to you in defense of this erroneous opinion. As for the thief, although in God's judgment he might be reckoned among those who are purified by the confession of martyrdom, yet you cannot tell whether he was not baptized. For, to say nothing of the opinion that he might have been sprinkled with the water which gushed at the same time with the blood out of the Lord's side, as he hung on the cross next to Him, and thus have been washed with a baptism of the most sacred kind, what if he had been baptized in prison, as in after times some under persecution were enabled privately to obtain? or what if he had been baptized prebefores imprisonment? If, indeed, he had been, the remission of his sins which he would have received in that case from God would not have protected him from the sentence of public law, so far as appertained to the death of the body. What if, being already baptized, he had committed the crime and incurred the punishment of robbery and lawlessness, but yet received, by virtue of repentance added to his baptism, forgiveness of the sins which, though baptized, he had committed? For beyond doubt his faith and piety appeared to the Lord clearly in his heart, as they do to us in his words. If, indeed, we were to conclude that all those who have quitted life without a record of their baptism died unbaptized, we should calumniate the very apostles themselves; for we are ignorant when they were, any of them, baptized, except the Apostle Paul. If, however, we could regard as an evidence that they were really baptized the circumstance of the Lord's saying to St. Peter, "He that is washed needed not save to wash his feet," what are we to think of the others, of whom we do not read even so much as this,—Barnabas, Timothy, Titus, Silas, Philemon, the very evangelists Mark and Luke, and innumerable others, about whose baptism God forbid that we should entertain any doubt, although we read no record of it? As for Dinocrates, he was a child of seven years of age; and as children who are baptized so old as that can now recite the creed and answer for themselves in the usual examination, I know not why he may not be supposed after his baptism to have been recalled by his unbelieving father to the sacrilege and profanity of heathen worship, and for this reason to have been condemned to the pains from which he was liberated at his sister's intercession. For in the account of him you have never read, either that he was never a Christian, or died a catechumen. But for the matter of that, the account itself that we have of him does not occur in that canon of Holy Scripture whence in all questions of this kind our proofs ought always to be drawn.

Chapter 13 [X]—His Seventh Error. (See Above in Book II. 13 [IX.].)

If you wish to be a catholic, do not venture to believe, to say, or to teach that "they whom the Lord has predestinated for baptism can be snatched away from his predestination, or die before that has been accomplished in them which the Almighty has predestined." There is in such a dogma more power than I can tell assigned to chances in opposition to the power of God, by the occurrence of which casualties that which He has predestinated is not permitted to come to pass. It is hardly necessary to spend time or earnest words in cautioning the man who takes up with this error against the absolute vortex of confusion into which it will absorb him, when I shall sufficiently meet the case if I briefly warn the prudent man who is ready to receive correction against the threatening mischief. Now these are your words: "We say that some such method as this must be had recourse to in the case of infants who, being predestinated for baptism, are yet, by the failing of this life, hurried away before they are born again in Christ." Is it then really true that any who have been predestinated to baptism are forestalled before they come to it by the failing of this life? And could God predestinate anything which He either in His foreknowledge saw would not come to pass, or in ignorance knew not that it could not come to pass, either to the frustration of His purpose or the discredit of His foreknowledge? You see how many weighty remarks might be made on this subject; but I am restrained by the fact of having treated on it a little while ago, so that I content myself with this brief and passing admonition.

Chapter 14. —His Eighth Error. (See Above in Book II. 13 [IX.].)

Refuse, if you wish to be a catholic, to believe, or to say, or to teach that "it is of infants, who are forestalled by death before they are born again in Christ, that the Scripture says, 'Speedily was he taken away, lest that wickedness should alter his understanding, or deceit beguile his soul. Therefore, God hastened to take him away from among the wicked; for his soul pleased the Lord; and being made perfect in a short time he fulfilled long seasons.'" For this passage has nothing to do with those to whom you apply it, but rather belongs to those who, after they have been baptized and have progressed in pious living, are not permitted to tarry long on earth, — having been made perfect, not with years, but with the grace of heavenly wisdom. This error however, of yours, by which you think that this scripture was spoken of infants who die unbaptized, does an intolerable wrong to the holy laver itself, if an infant, who could have been "hurried away" after baptism, has been "hurried away" before this, for this reason: — "lest wickedness should alter his understanding, or deceit beguile his soul." As if this "wickedness," and this "deceit which beguiles the soul," and changes it for the worse, if it be not before taken away, is to be believed to be in baptism itself! In a word, since his soul had pleased God, He hastened to remove him out of the midst of iniquity; and he tarried not for ever so little while, in order to fulfil in him what He had predestinated; but preferred to act in opposition to His predestined purpose, and actually hastened lest what had pleased Him so well in the unbaptized child should be exterminated by his baptism! As if the dying infant would perish in that, whither we ought to run with him in our arms in order to save him from perdition. Who, therefore, in respect of these words of the Book of Wisdom, could believe, or say, or write, or quote them as having been written concerning infants who die without baptism, if he only reflected upon them with proper consideration?

Chapter 15 [XI.]—His Ninth Error. (See Above in Book II. 14 [X.].)

If you wish to be a catholic, I pray you, neither believe, nor say, nor teach that "there are some mansions outside the kingdom of God which the Lord said were in His Father's house." For He does not affirm, as you have adduced his testimony, "There are with my Father (apud Patrem meum) many mansions;" although, if He had even expressed Himself so, the mansions could hardly be supposed to have any other situation than in the house of His Father; but He plainly says, "In my Father's house are many mansions." Now, who would be so reckless as to separate some parts of God's house from the kingdom of God; so that, whilst the kings of the earth are found reigning, not in their house only, nor only in their own country, but far and wide, even in regions across the sea, the King who made the heaven and the earth is not described as reigning even over all His own house?

Chapter 16. —God Rules Everywhere: and Yet the "Kingdom of Heaven" May Not Be Everywhere.

You may, however, not improbably contend that all things, it is true, belong to the kingdom of God, because He reigns in heaven, reigns on earth, in the depths beneath, in paradise, in hell (for where does He not reign, since His power is everywhere supreme?); but that the kingdom of heaven is one thing, into which none are permitted to enter, according to the Lord's own true and settled sentence, unless they are washed in the laver of regeneration, while quite another thing is the kingdom over the earth, or over any other parts of creation, in which there may be some mansions of God's house; but these, although appertaining to the kingdom of God, belong not to that kingdom of heaven where God's kingdom exists with an especial excellence and blessedness; and that it hence happens that, while no parts and mansions of God's house can be rudely separated from the kingdom of God, yet not all the mansions are prepared in the kingdom of heaven; and still, even in the abodes which are not situated in the kingdom of heaven, those may live happily, to whom, if they are even unbaptized, God has willed to assign such habitations. They are no doubt in the kingdom of God, although (as not having been baptized) they cannot possibly be in the kingdom of heaven.

Chapter 17. —Where the Kingdom of God May Be Understood to Be.

Now, they who say this, do no doubt seem to themselves to say a good deal, because theirs is only a slight and careless view of Scripture; nor do they understand in what sense we use the phrase, "kingdom of God," when we say of it in our prayers, "Thy kingdom come;" for that is called the kingdom of God, in which His whole family shall reign with Him in happiness and forever. Now, in respect of the power which He possesses over all things, he is of course even now reigning. What, therefore, do we intend when we pray that His kingdom may come unless that we may deserve to reign with Him? But even they will be under His power who shall have to suffer the pains of eternal fire. Well, then, do we mean to predicate of these unhappy beings that they too will be in the kingdom of God? Surely it is one thing to be honored with the gifts and privileges of the kingdom of God, and another thing to be restrained and punished by the laws of the same. However, that you may have a very manifest proof that on the one hand the kingdom of heaven must not be parceled out to the baptized, and other portions of the kingdom of God be given to the unbaptized, as you seem to have determined, I beg of you to hear the Lord's own words; He does not say, "Except a man be born again of water and of the Spirit, he cannot enter into the kingdom of heaven;" but His words are, "he cannot enter into the kingdom of God." His discourse with Nicodemus on the subject before us runs thus: "Verily, verily, I say unto thee, Except a man be born again, he cannot see the kingdom of God." Observe, He does not here say, the kingdom of heaven, but the kingdom of God. And then, on Nicodemus asking Him in reply, "How can a man be born when he is old? can he enter the second time into his mother's womb and be born?" the Lord, in explanation, repeats His former statement more plainly and openly: "Verily, verily, I say unto you, Except a man be born again of water and of the Spirit, he cannot enter into the kingdom of God." Observe again, He uses the same phrase, the kingdom of God, not the kingdom of heaven. It is worthy of remark, that while He varies two expressions in explaining them the second time (for after saying, "Except a man be born again," He interprets that by the fuller expression, "Except a man be born of water and the Spirit;" and in like manner He explains, "he cannot see," by the completer phrase, "he cannot enter into"), He yet makes no variation here; He said "the kingdom of God" the first time, and He afterwards repeated the same phrase exactly. It is not now necessary to raise and discuss the question, whether the kingdom of God and the kingdom of heaven must be understood as involving different senses, or whether only one thing is described under two designations. It is enough to find that no one can enter into the kingdom of God, except he be washed in the laver of regeneration. I suppose you perceive by this time how wide of the truth it is to separate from the kingdom of God any mansions that are placed in the house of God. And as to the idea which you have entertained that there will be found dwelling among the various mansions, which the Lord has told us abound in His Father's house, some who have not been born again of water and the Spirit, I advise you, if you will permit me, not to defer amending it, in order that you may hold the catholic faith.

Chapter 18 [XII.]—His Tenth Error. (See Above in Book I. 13 [XI.] and Book II. 15 [XI.]).

Again, if you wish to be a catholic, I pray you, neither believe, nor say, nor teach that "the sacrifice of Christians ought to be offered in behalf of those who have departed out of the body without having been baptized." Because you fail to show that the sacrifice of the Jews, which you have quoted out of the books of the Maccabees, was offered in behalf of any who had departed this life without circumcision. In this novel opinion of yours, which you have advanced against the authority and teaching of the whole Church, you have used a very arrogant mode of expression. You say, "In behalf of these, I most certainly decide that constant oblations and incessant sacrifices must be offered up on the part of the holy priests." Here you show, as a layman, no submission to God's priests for instruction; nor do you associate yourself with them (the least you could do) for inquiry; but you put yourself before them by your proud assumption of judgment. Away, my son, with all this pretension; men walk not so arrogantly in the Way, which the Humble Christ taught that He Himself is. No man enters through His narrow gate with so proud a disposition as this.

Chapter 19 [XIII.]—His Eleventh Error. (See Above in Book I. 15 [XII.] and Book II. 16.)

Once more, if you desire to be a catholic, do not believe, or say, or teach that "some of those persons who have departed this life without Christ's baptism, do not in the meantime go into the kingdom of heaven, but into paradise; yet afterwards in the resurrection of the dead they attain also to the blessedness of the kingdom of heaven." Even the Pelagian heresy was not daring enough to grant them this, although it holds that infants do not contract original sin. You, however, as a catholic, confess that they are born in sin; and yet by some unaccountable perverseness in the novel opinion you put forth, you assert that they are absolved from that sin with which they were born, and admitted into the kingdom of heaven without the baptism which saves. Nor do you seem to be aware how much below Pelagius himself you are in your views on this point. For he, being alarmed by that sentence of the Lord which does not permit unbaptized persons to enter into the kingdom of heaven, does not venture to send infants thither, although he believes them to be free from all sin; whereas you have so little regard for what is written, "Except a man be born again of water and of the Spirit, he cannot enter into the kingdom of God," that (to say nothing of the error which induces you recklessly to sever paradise from the kingdom of God) you do not hesitate to promise to certain persons, whom you, as a catholic, believe to be born under guilt, both absolution from this guilt and the kingdom of heaven, even when they die without baptism. As if you could possibly be a true catholic because you build up the doctrine of original sin against Pelagius, if you show yourself a new heretic against the Lord, by pulling down His statement respecting baptism. For our own part, beloved brother, we do not desire thus to gain victories over heretics: vanquishing one error by another, and, what is still worse, a less one by a greater. You say, "Should anyone perhaps be reluctant to allow that paradise was temporarily bestowed in the meantime on the souls of the dying thief and of Dinocrates, while there still remains to them the reversion of the kingdom of heaven at the resurrection, seeing that the principal passage stands in the way of the opinion, 'Except a man be born again of water and the Holy Spirit, he cannot enter into the kingdom of heaven,' he may still hold my ungrudging assent on this point; only let him do full honor to both the effect and the aim of the divine mercy and foreknowledge." These are your own words, and in them you express your agreement with the man who says that paradise is conferred on certain unbaptized for a time, in such a sense that at the resurrection there is in store for them the reward of the kingdom of heaven, in opposition to "that principal passage" which has determined that none shall enter into that kingdom who has not been born again of water and the Holy Ghost. Pelagius was afraid to oppose himself to this "principal passage" of the Gospel, and he did not believe that any (whom he still did not supposed to be sinners) would enter into the kingdom of heaven unbaptized. You, on the contrary, acknowledge that infants have original sin, and yet you absolve them from it without the laver of regeneration, and send them for a temporary residence in paradise, and subsequently permit them to enter even into the kingdom of heaven.

Chapter 20 [XIV.]—Augustin Calls on Victor to Correct His Errors. (See Above in Book II. 22 [XVI.].)

Now these errors, and such as these, with whatever others you may perhaps be able to discover in your books on a more attentive and leisurely perusal, I beg of you to correct, if you possess a catholic mind; in other words, if you spoke in perfect sincerity when you said, that you were not over-confident in yourself that what statements you had made were all capable of proof; and that your constant aim was not to maintain even your own opinion, if it were shown to be improbable; and that it gave you much pleasure, if your own judgment were condemned, to adopt and pursue better and truer sentiments. Well now, my dear brother, show that you said this in no fallacious sense; so that the catholic Church may rejoice in your capacity and character, as possessing not only genius, but prudence withal, and piety, and moderation, rather than that the madness of heresy should be kindled by your contentious persistence in these errors. Now you have an opportunity of showing also how sincerely you expressed your feelings in the passage which immediately follows the satisfactory statement which I have just now mentioned of yours. "For," you say, "as it is the mark of every highest aim and laudable purpose to transfer one's self readily to truer views; so it shows a depraved and obstinate judgment to refuse to return promptly to the pathway of reason." Well, then, show yourself to be influenced by this high aim and laudable purpose, and transfer your mind readily to truer views; and do not display a depraved and obstinate judgment by refusing to return promptly to the pathway of reason. For if your words were uttered in frank sincerity, if they were not mere sound of the lips, if you really felt them in your heart, then you cannot but abhor all delay in accomplishing the great good of correcting yourself. It was not, indeed, much for you to allow, that it showed a depraved and obstinate judgment to refuse to return to the pathway of reason, unless you had added "promptly." By adding this, you showed us how execrable is his conduct who never accomplishes the reform; since even he who effects it but tardily appears to you to deserve so severe a censure, as to be fairly described as displaying a depraved and obstinate mind. Listen, therefore, to your own admonition, and turn to good account mainly and largely the fruitful resources of your eloquence; that so you may promptly return to the pathway of reason, more promptly, indeed, than when you declined therefrom, at an unstable period of your age, when you were fortified with too little prudence and less learning.

Chapter 21. —Augustin Compliments Victor's Talents and Diligence.

It would take me too long a time to handle and discuss fully all the points which I wish to be amended in your books, or rather in your own self, and to give you even a brief reason for the correction of each particular. And yet you must not because of them despise yourself, so as to suppose that your ability and powers of speech are to be thought lightly of. I have discovered in you no small recollection of the sacred Scriptures; but your erudition is less than was proportioned to your talent, and the labor you bestowed on them. My desire, therefore, is that you should not, on the one hand, grow vain by attributing too much to yourself; nor, on the other hand, become cold and indifferent by prostration or despair. I only wish that I could read your writings in company with yourself, and point out the necessary emendations in conversation rather than by writing. This is a matter which could be more easily accomplished by oral communication between ourselves than in letters. If the entire subject were to be treated in writing, it would require many volumes. Those chief errors, however, which I have wished to sum up comprehensively in a definite number, I at once call your attention to, in order that you may not postpone the correction of them, but banish them entirely from your preaching and belief; so that the great faculty which you possess of disputation, may, by God's grace, be employed by you usefully for edification, not for injuring and destroying sound and wholesome doctrine.

Chapter 22 [XV.]—A Summary Recapitulation of the Errors of Victor.

What these particular errors are, I have, to the best of my ability, already explained. But I will run over them again with a brief recapitulation. One is, "That God did not make the soul out of nothing, but out of His own self." A second is, that "just as God who gives is Himself ever existent, so is He ever giving souls through infinite time." The third is, that "the soul lost some merit by the flesh, which it had had before the flesh." The fourth is, that "the soul by means of the flesh recovers its ancient condition, and is born again through the very same flesh by which it had deserved to be polluted." The fifth is, that "the soul deserved to be sinful, before any sin." The sixth is, that "infants which are forestalled by death before they are baptized, may yet attain to forgiveness of their original sins." The seventh is, that "they whom the Lord has predestinated to be baptized may be taken away from his predestination, or die before that has been accomplished in them which the Almighty has predestined." The eighth is, that "it is of infants who are fore-stalled by death, before they are born again in Christ, that the Scripture says, 'Speedily was he taken away, lest wickedness should alter his understanding,'" with the remainder of the passage to the same effect in the Book of Wisdom. The ninth is, that "there are outside the kingdom of God some of those mansions which the Lord said were in His Father's house." The tenth is, that "the sacrifice of Christians ought to be offered in behalf of those who have departed out of the body without being baptized." The eleventh is, that "some of those persons who have departed this life without the baptism of Christ do not in the meanwhile go into the kingdom, but into paradise; afterwards, however, in the resurrection of the dead, they attain even to the blessedness of the kingdom of heaven."

Chapter 23. —Obstinacy Makes the Heretic.

Well, now, as for these eleven propositions, they are extremely and manifestly perverse and opposed to the catholic faith; so that you should no longer hesitate to root them out and cast them away from your mind, from your words, and from your pen, if you are desirous that we should rejoice not only at your having come over to our catholic altars, but at your being really and truly a catholic. For if these dogmas of yours are severally maintained with pertinacity, they may possibly engender as many heresies as they number opinions. Wherefore consider, I pray you, how dreadful it is that they should be all concentrated in one person, when they would, if held severally by various persons, be every one of them damnable in each holder. If, however, you would in your own person cease to fight contentiously in their defense, nay, would turn your arms against them by faithful words and writings, you would acquire more praise as the censurer of your own self than if you directed any amount of right criticism against any other person; and your amendment of your own errors would bring you more admiration than if you had never entertained them. May the Lord be present to your heart and mind, and by His Spirit pour into your soul such readiness in humility, such light of truth, such sweetness of love, and such peaceful piety, that you may prefer being a conqueror of your own spirit in the truth, than of anyone else who gainsays it with his errors. But I do not by any means wish you to think, that by holding these opinions you have departed from the catholic faith, although they are unquestionably opposed to the catholic faith; if so be you are able, in the presence of that God whose eye infallibly searches every man's heart, to look back on your own words as being truly and sincerely expressed, when you said that you were not over-confident in yourself as to the opinions you had broached, that they were all capable of proof; and that your constant aim was not to persist in your own sentiments, if they were shown to be improbable; inasmuch as it was a real pleasure to you, when any judgment of yours was condemned, to adopt and pursue better and truer thoughts. Now such a temper as this, even in relation to what may have been said in an uncatholic form through ignorance, is itself catholic by the very purpose and readiness of amendment which it premeditates. With this remark, however, I must now end this volume, where the reader may rest a while, ready to renew his attention to what is to follow, when I begin my next book.

Book IV.

ADDRESSED TO VINCENTIUS VICTOR.

He first shows, that his hesitation about the origin of souls was undeservedly blamed, and that he was wrongly compared with cattle, because he had refrained from any rash conclusions on the subject. Then, again, about his own unhesitating statement, that the soul was spirit, not body, he points out how rashly Victor disapproved of this assertion, especially when he was vainly expending his efforts to prove that the soul was corporeal in its own nature, and that the spirit in man was distinct from the soul itself.

Chapter 1 [I.]—The Personal Character of This Book.

I Must now, in the sequel of my treatise, request you to hear what I desire to say to you concerning myself—as I best can; or rather as He shall enable me in whose hand are both ourselves and our words. For you blamed me on two several occasions, even going so far as to mention my name. In the beginning of your book you spoke of yourself as being perfectly conscious of your own want of skill, and as being destitute of the support of learning; and, when you mentioned me, bestowed on me the complimentary phrases of "most learned" and "most skillful." But yet, all the while, on those subjects in which you seemed to yourself to be perfectly acquainted with what I either confess my ignorance of, or presume with no unbecoming liberty to have some knowledge of, you—young as you are, and a layman too—did not hesitate to censure me, an old man and a bishop, and a person withal whom in your own judgment you had pronounced most learned and most skillful. Well, for my own part, I know nothing about my great learning and skill; nay, I am very certain that I possess no such eminent qualities; moreover, I have no doubt that it is quite within the scope of possibility, that it may fall to the lot of even an unskillful and unlearned man occasionally to know what a learned and skillful person is ignorant of; and in this I plainly commend you, that you have preferred to merely personal regard a love of truth,—for if you have not understood the truth, yet at any rate you have thought it such. This you have done no doubt with temerity, because you thought you knew what you were really ignorant of; and without restraint, because, having no respect of persons, you chose to publish abroad whatever was in your mind. You ought therefore to understand how much greater our care should be to recall the Lord's sheep from their errors; since it is evidently wrong for even the sheep to conceal from the shepherds whatever faults they have discovered in them. O that you censured me in such things as are indeed worthy of just blame! For I must not deny that both in my conduct and in my writings there are many points which may be censured by a sound judge without temerity. Now, if you would select any of these for your censure, I might be able by them to show you how I should like you to behave in those particulars which you judiciously and fairly condemned; moreover, I should have (as an elder to a younger, and as one in authority to him who must obey) an opportunity of setting you an example under correction which should not be humbler on my part than wholesome to both of us. With respect, however, to the points on which you have actually censured me, they are not such as humility obliges me to correct, but such as truth compels me partly to acknowledge and partly to defend.

Chapter 2 [II.]—The Points Which Victor Thought Blameworthy in Augustin.

And they are these: The first, that I did not venture to make a definite statement touching the origin of those souls which have been given, or are being given, to human beings, since the first man—because I confess my ignorance of the subject; the second, because I said I was sure the soul was spirit, not body. Under this second point, however, you have included two grounds of censure: one, because I refused to believe the soul to be corporeal; the other, because I affirmed it to be spirit. For to you the soul appears both to be body and not to be spirit. I must therefore request your attention to my own defense against your censure, and ask you to embrace the opportunity which my self-defense affords you of learning what points there are in yourself also which require your amendment. Recall, then, the words of your book in which you first mentioned my name. "I know," you say, "many men of very great reputation who when consulted have kept silence, or admitted nothing clearly, but have withdrawn from their discussions everything definite when they commence their exposition. Of such character are the contents of sundry writings which I have read at your house by a very learned man and renowned bishop, called Augustin. The truth is, I suppose, they have with an overweening modesty and diffidence investigated the mysteries of this subject, and have consumed within themselves the judgment of their own treatises, and have professed themselves incapable of determining anything on this point. But, I assure you, it appears to me excessively absurd and unreasonable that a man should be a stranger to himself; or that a person who is supposed to have acquired the knowledge of all things, should regard himself as unknown to his very self. For what difference is there between a man and a brute beast, if he knows not how to discuss and determine his own quality and nature? so that there may justly be applied to him the statement of Scripture: 'Man, although he was in honor, understood not; he is like the cattle, and is compared with them.' For when the good and gracious God created everything with reason and wisdom, and produced man as a rational animal, capable of understanding, endowed with reason, and lively with sensation, —because by His prudent arrangement He assigns their place to all creatures which do not participate in the faculty of reason, —what more incongruous idea could be suggested, than that God had withheld from him the simple knowledge of himself? The wisdom of this world, indeed, is ever aiming with much effort to attain to the knowledge of truth; its researches, no doubt, fall short of the aim, from its inability to know through what agency it is permitted that truth should be ascertained; but yet there are some things on the nature of the soul, near (I might even say, akin) to the truth which it has attempted to discern. Under these circumstances, how unbecoming and even shameful a thing it is, that any man of religious principle should either have no intelligent views on this very subject, or prohibit himself from acquiring any!"

Chapter 3. —How Much Do We Know of the Nature of the Body?

Well, now, this extremely lucid and eloquent castigation which you have inflicted on our ignorance lays you so strictly under the necessity of knowing every possible thing which appertains to the nature of man, that, should you unhappily be ignorant of any particular, you must (and remember it is not I, but you, that have made the necessity) be compared with "the cattle." For although you appear to aim your censure at us more especially, when you quote the passage, "Man, although he was in honor, understood not," inasmuch as we (unlike yourself) hold an honorable place in the Church; yet even you occupy too honorable a rank in nature, not to be preferred above the cattle, with which according to your own judgment you will have to be compared, if you should happen to be ignorant on any of the points which manifestly appertain to your nature. For you have not merely aspersed with your censure those who are affected with the same ignorance as I am myself laboring under, that is to say, concerning the origin of the human soul (although I am not indeed absolutely ignorant even on this point, for I know that God breathed into the face of the first man, and that "man then became a living soul,"—a truth, however, which I could never have known by myself, unless I had read of it in the Scripture); but you asked in so many words, "What difference is there between a man and a brute beast, if he knows not how to discuss and determine his own quality and nature?" And you seem to have entertained your opinion so distinctly, as to have thought that a man ought to be able to discuss and determine the facts of his own entire quality and nature so clearly, that nothing concerning himself should escape his observation. Now, if this is really the truth of the matter, I must now compare you to "the cattle," if you cannot tell me the precise number of the hairs of your head. But if, however far we may advance in this life, you allow us to be ignorant of sundry facts appertaining to our nature, I then want to know how far your concession extends, lest, perchance, it may include the very point we are now raising, that we do not by any means know the origin of our soul; although we know,—a thing which belongs to faith,—beyond all doubt, that the soul is a gift to man from God, and that it still is not of the same nature as God Himself. Do you, moreover, think that each person's ignorance of his own nature must be exactly on the same level as your ignorance of it? Must everybody's knowledge, too, of the subject be equal to what you have been able to attain to? So that if he is so unfortunate as to possess a slightly larger amount of ignorance than yourself, you must compare him with cattle; and on the same principle, if any one shall be ever so little wiser than yourself on this subject, he will have the pleasure of comparing you with equal justice to the aforesaid cattle. I must therefore request you to tell me, to what extent you permit us to be ignorant of our nature so as to save our distance from the formidable cattle; and I beg you besides duly to reflect, whether he is not further removed from cattle who knows his ignorance of any part of the subject, than he is who thinks he knows what in fact he knows not. The entire nature of man is certainly spirit, soul, and body; therefore, whoever would alienate the body from man's nature, is unwise. Those medical men, however, who are called anatomists have investigated with careful scrutiny, by dissecting processes, even living men, so far as men have been able to retain any life in the hands of the examiners; their researches have penetrated limbs, veins, nerves, bones, marrow, the internal vitals; and all to discover the nature of the body. But none of these men have ever thought of comparing us with the cattle, because of our ignorance of their subject. But perhaps you will say that it is those who are ignorant of the nature of the soul, not of the body, who are to be compared with the brute beasts. Then you ought not to have expressed yourself at starting in the way you have done. Your words are not, "For what difference is there between a man and cattle, if he is ignorant of the nature and quality of the soul;" but you say, "if he knows not how to discuss and determine his own nature and quality." Of course, our quality and our nature must be taken account of together with the body, but at the same time the investigation of the several elements of which we are composed is conducted in each case separately. For my own part, indeed, if I wished to display how far it was in my power to treat scientifically and intelligently the entire field of man's nature, I should have to fill many volumes; not to mention how many topics there are which I must confess my ignorance of.

Chapter 4 [III.]—Is the Question of Breath One that Concerns the Soul, or Body, or What?

But to what, in your judgment, does that which we discussed in our former book concerning the breath of man belong?—to the nature of the soul, seeing that it is the soul which effects it in man; or to that of the body, since the body is moved by the soul to effect it; or to that of this air, by whose alternation of action it is discovered to effect it; or rather to all three, that is to say, to the soul as that which moves the body, and to the body which by its motion receives and emits the breath, and also to the circumambient air which raises by its entrance, and by its departure depresses? And yet you were evidently ignorant of all this, learned and eloquent though you are, when you supposed, and said, and wrote, and read in the presence of the crowd assembled to hear your opinion, that it was out of our own nature that we inflated a bag, and yet had no diminution of our nature at all by the operation; although you might most easily ascertain how we accomplish the process, not by any tedious examination of the pages either of human or of inspired writings, but by a simple investigation of your own physical action, whenever you liked. This, then, being the case, how can I trust you to teach me concerning the origin of souls, —a subject which I confess myself to be ignorant of, —you who are actually ignorant of what you are doing unintermittingly with your nose and mouth, and of why you are doing it? May the Lord bring it to pass that you may be advised by me, and accept rather than resist so manifest a truth, and one so ready to your hand. May you also not interrogate your lungs about the bag inflation in such a temper as to prefer inflating them in opposition to me, rather than acquiesce in their tuition, when they answer your inquiry with entire truth, —not by speech and altercation, but by breath and respiration. Then I could bear with you patiently while you correct and reproach me for my ignorance of the origin of souls; nay, I could even warmly thank you, if, besides inflicting on me rebuke, you would convince me with truth. For if you could teach me the truth I am ignorant of, it would be my duty to bear with all patience any blows you might deal against me, not in word only, but even with hand.

Chapter 5 [IV.]—God Alone Can Teach Whence Souls Come.

Now with respect to the question between us, I confess to your loving self I greatly desire to know one of two things if I can, —either concerning the origin of souls, of which I am ignorant, or whether this knowledge is within our reach so long as we are in the present life. For what if our controversy touches the very points of which it is enjoined to us, "Seek not out the things that are too high for thee, neither search the things that are above thy strength; but whatever things the Lord hath commanded and taught thee, think thereupon for evermore." This, then, is what I desire to know, either from God Himself, who knows what He creates, or even from some competently learned man who knows what he is saying, not from a person who is ignorant of the breath he heaves. It is not everybody who recollects his own infancy; and do you suppose that a man is able, without divine instruction, to know whence he began to exist in his mother's womb, —especially if the knowledge of human nature has so completely eluded him as to leave him ignorant, not only of what is within him, but of that also which is added to his nature from without? Will you, my dearest brother, be able to teach me, or anyone else, whence human beings at their birth are ensouled, when you still know not how it is that their life is so sustained by food, that they are certain to die if the aliment is withdrawn for a while? Or will you be able to teach me, or anyone else, whence men obtain their souls, when you are still actually ignorant whence bags, when inflated, get the filling? My only wish, as you are ignorant whence souls have their origin, is, that I may on my side know whether such knowledge is attainable by me in this present life. If this be one of the things which are too high for us, and which we are forbidden to seek out or search into, then we have good grounds for fearing lest we should sin, not by our ignorance of it, but our quest after it. For we ought not to suppose that a subject, to fall under the category of the things which are too high for us, must appertain to the nature of God, and not to our own.

Chapter 6 [V.]—Questions About the Nature of the Body are Sufficiently Mysterious, and Yet Not Higher Than Those of the Soul.

What do you say to the statement, that amongst the works of God there are some which it is more difficult to know than even God Himself, —so far, indeed, as He can be an object of knowledge to us at all? For we have learnt that God is a Trinity; but to this very day we do not know how many kinds of animals, not even of land animals which were able to enter Noah's ark, He has created—unless by some happy chance you have ascertained this fact. Again, in the Book of Wisdom it is written, "For if they could prevail so much, that they could know and estimate the world; how is it that they did not more easily find out the Lord thereof?" Is it because the subject before us is within us that it is therefore not too high for us? For it must be granted that the nature of our soul is a more internal thing than our body. As if the soul has been no better able to explore the body itself externally by the eyes of that body than internally by its own means. For what is there in the inward parts of the body where the soul does not exist? But yet, even about these several inner and vital portions of our frame, the soul has examined and searched them out by the bodily eyes; and all that it has succeeded in learning of them it has acquired by means of the eyes of the body; and, without doubt, all the material substance was there, even when the soul knew not of it. Since also our inward parts are incapable of living without the soul, it follows that the soul has been more able to give them life than to know them. Well, then, is the soul's body a higher object for its knowledge than the soul's own self? And therefore if it wishes to inquire and consider when human seed is converted into blood, when into solid flesh; when the bones begin to harden, and when to fill with marrow; how many kinds of veins and nerves there are; by what channels and circuits the former serve for irrigation and the latter for ligature to the entire body; whether the skin is to be reckoned among the nerves, and the teeth among the bones,—for they show some difference, inasmuch as they have no marrow; and in what respect the nails differ from both, being similar to them in hardness, while they possess a quality in common with the hair, in being capable of growing and being cut; what, again, is the use of those veins wherein air, instead of blood, circulates, which they call the arteries—if, I repeat, the soul desired to come to know these and similar points respecting the nature of its body, ought it then to be said to a man, "Seek not out the things that are too high for thee, neither search the things that are above thy strength?" But, if the inquiry be made into the soul's own origin, of which subject it knows nothing, the matter then, forsooth, is not too high or beyond one's strength to be capable of apprehension? And you deem it an absurd thing, and incompatible with reason, for the soul not to know whether it is inbreathed by God, or whether it is derived from the parents, although it does not remember this event as soon as it is past, and reckons it among the things which it has forgotten beyond recall, —like infancy, and all other stages of life which followed close upon birth, though doubtless, when they happened, they were not unaccompanied with sensation. But yet you do not deem it absurd or unreasonable that it should be ignorant of the body which is subject to it, and should know nothing whatever about incidents pertaining to it which are not in the category of things that are past, but of present facts, —as to whether it sets the veins in motion in order to produce life in the body, but the nerves in order to operate by the limbs of the body; and if so, why it does not move the nerves except at its especial will, whereas it affects the pulsations of the veins without intermission, even without willing; from what part of the body that which they call the ἡγεμονικόν(the authoritative part of the soul, the reason) exercises its universal rule, whether from the heart or from the brain, or by a distribution, the motions from the heart and the sensations from the brain,—or from the brain, both the sensations and voluntary motions, but from the heart, the involuntary pulsations of the veins; and once more, if it does both of these from the brain, how is it that it has the sensations, even without willing, while it does not move the limbs except it wills? Inasmuch, then, as only the soul itself does all this in the body, how is it that it knows not what it does? or whence its power to do it? And it is no disgrace to it to be so ignorant. Then do you suppose it to be a discredit if it knows not whence or how it was itself made, since it certainly did not make itself? Well, then, none know how or whence the soul effects all its action in the body; do you not therefore think that it, too, appertains to those things which are said to be "too high for us, and above our strength"?

Chapter 7 [VI.]—We Often Need More Teaching as to What is Most Intimately Ours Than as to What is Further from Us.

But I must put to you a far wider question arising out of our subject. Why should only a very few know why all men do what they do? Perhaps you will tell me, Because they have learnt the art of anatomy or experiment, which are both comprised in the physician's education, which few obtain, while others have refused to acquire the information, although they might, of course, if they had liked. Here, then, I say nothing of the point why many try to acquire this information, but cannot, because they are hindered by a slow intellect (which, however, is a very strange fact) from learning of others what is done by their own selves and in their own selves. But this is a very important question which I now ask, Why I should have no need of art to know that there is a sun in the heavens, and a moon, and other stars; but must have the aid of art to know, on moving my finger, whence the act begins,—from the heart, or the brain, or from both, or from neither: why I do not require a teacher to know what is so much higher than me; but must yet wait for someone else to learn whence that is done by me which is done within me? For although we are said to think in our heart, and although we know what our thoughts are, without the knowledge of any other person, yet we know not in what part of the body we have the heart itself, where we do our thinking, unless we are taught it by some other person, who yet is ignorant of what we think. I am not unaware that when we hear that we should love God with our whole heart, this is not said of that portion of our flesh which lies under our ribs, but of that power that originates our thoughts. And this is properly designated by this name, because, as motion does not cease in the heart whence the pulsation of the veins radiates in every direction, so in the process of thought we do not rest in the act itself and abstain from further pondering. But although every sensation is imparted even to the body by the soul, how is it that we can count our external limbs, even in the dark and with closed eyes, by the bodily sense which is called "touch," but we know nothing of our internal functions in the very central region of the soul itself, where that power is present which imparts life and animation to all else,—a mystery this which, I apprehend, no medical men of any kind, whether empirics, or anatomists, or dogmatists, or methodists, or any man living, have any knowledge of?

Chapter 8. —We Have No Memory of Our Creation.

And whosoever shall have attempted to fathom such knowledge may not improperly have addressed to him the words we have before quoted, "Seek not out the things that are too high for thee, neither search the things that are above thy strength." Now it is not a question of mere altitude, such as is beyond our stature, but it is an elevation which our intelligence cannot reach, and a strength which our mental power cannot cope with. And yet it is neither the heaven of heavens, nor the measure of the stars, nor the scope of sea and land, nor the nethermost hell; it is our own selves that we are incapable of comprehending; it is our own selves, who, in our too great height and strength, transcend the humble limits of our own knowledge; it is our own selves, whom we are incapable of embracing, although we are certainly not beside ourselves. But we are not to be compared with cattle simply because we do not perfectly discover what we ourselves are: and yet you think that we deserve the humiliating comparison, if we have forgotten what we were, even though we knew it once. My soul is not now being derived from my parents, is not now receiving insufflation from God. Whichever of these two processes He used, He used when He created me; He is not at this moment using it of me, or within me. It is past and gone, —not a present thing, nor a recent one to me. I do not even know whether I was aware of it and then forgot it; or whether I was unable, even at the time when it was done, to feel and to know it.

Chapter 9 [VII.]—Our Ignorance of Ourselves Illustrated by the Remarkable Memory of One Simplicius.

Observe now, while we are, while we live, while we know that we live, while we are certain that we possess memory, understanding, and will; who boast of ourselves as having a great knowledge of our own nature; —observe, I say, how entirely ignorant we are of what avail to us is our memory, or our understanding, or our will. A certain man who from his youth has been a friend of mine, named Simplicius, is a person of accurate and astonishing memory. I once asked him to tell me what were the last lines but one of all the books of Virgil; he immediately answered my question without the least hesitation, and with perfect accuracy. I then asked him to repeat the preceding lines; he did so. And I really believe that he could have repeated Virgil line after line backward. For wherever I wished, I made trial whether he could do it, and he did it. Similarly in prose, from any of Cicero's orations, which he had learnt by heart, he would perform a similar feat at our request, by reciting backwards as far as we wished. Upon our expressing astonishment, he called God to witness that he had no idea of this ability of his before that trial. So far, therefore, as memory is concerned, his mind only then learnt its own power; and such discovery would at no time be possible except by trial and experiment. Moreover, he was of course the very same man before he tried his powers; how was it, then, that he was ignorant of himself?

Chapter 10. —The Fidelity of Memory; The Unsearchable Treasure of Memory; The Powers of a Man's Understanding Sufficiently Understood by None.

We often assume that we shall retain a thing in our memory; and so thinking, we do not write it down. But afterwards, when we wish to recall it, it refuses to come to mind; and we are then sorry that we thought it would return to memory, or that we did not secure it in writing so as to prevent its escape; and lo, on a sudden, without our seeking it, it occurs to us. Then does it follow that we were not ourselves when we thought this? And that we cease to be the same thing that we were, when we are no longer able to think it? Now how does it happen that I know not how we are abstracted from, and denied to, ourselves; and similarly am ignorant how we are restored and returned to ourselves? As if we are other persons, and elsewhere, when we seek, but fail to find, what we deposited in our memory; and are ourselves incapable of returning to ourselves, as if we were situated somewhere else; but afterwards return again, on finding ourselves out. For where do we make our quest, except in our own selves? And what is it we search for, except our own selves? As if we were not actually at home in our persons, but had gone some whither. Do you not observe, even with alarm, so deep a mystery? And what is all this but our own nature—not what it has been, but such as it now is? And observe how much more we seek than we comprehend. I have often believed that I could understand a question which had been submitted to me, if I were to bestow thought upon it. Well, I have bestowed the thought, but have not been able to solve the question; and many a time I have not so believed, and yet have been able to determine the point. The powers, then, of my own understanding have not been really known to me; nor, I apprehend, have they been to you either.

Chapter 11. —The Apostle Peter Told No Lie, When He Said He Was Ready to Lay Down His Life for the Lord, But Only Was Ignorant of His Will.

But perhaps you despise me for confessing all this, and will in consequence compare me with "cattle." For myself, however, I will not cease to advise you, or (if you refuse to listen to me) at all events to warn you, to acknowledge rather this common infirmity, in which virtue is perfected; lest, by assuming unknown things to be known, you fail to attain to the truth. For I suppose that there is something which even you wish to understand, but are unable; which you would never seek to understand, unless you hoped someday to succeed in your research. Thus, you also are ignorant of the powers of your own understanding, who profess to know all about your own nature, and decline to follow me in my confession of ignorance. Well, there is also the will; what am I to say about that, where certainly free choice is ostentatiously claimed by us? The blessed Apostle Peter, indeed, was willing to lay down his life for the Lord. He was no doubt sincere in his willingness; nor was he treacherous to the Lord when he made the promise. But his will was entirely ignorant of its own powers. Therefore the great apostle, who had discovered his Master to be the Son of God, was unknown to himself.

Thus, we are quite aware respecting ourselves that we will a thing, or "nil" it; but although our will is a good one, we are ignorant, my dear son, unless we deceive ourselves, of its strength, of its resources, of what temptations it may yield to, or of what it may resist.

Chapter 12 [VIII.]—The Apostle Paul Could Know the Third Heaven and Paradise, But Not Whether He Was in the Body or Not.

See therefore how many facts of our nature, not of the past but of the present time, and not pertaining to the body only, but also to our inner man, we know nothing about, without deserving to be compared with the brute beasts. And yet this is the opprobrious comparison which you have thought me worthy of, because I have not complete knowledge of the past origin of my soul—although I am not wholly ignorant of it, since I know that it was given me by God, and yet that it is not out of God. But when can I enumerate all the particulars relating to the nature of our spirit and our soul of which we are ignorant? Whereas we ought rather to utter that exclamation before God, which the Psalmist uttered: "The knowledge of Thee is too wonderful for me; it is very difficult, I cannot attain to it." Now why did he add the words for me, except because he conjectured how incomprehensible was the knowledge of God for himself, since he was unable to comprehend even his own self? The apostle was caught up into the third heaven, and heard unspeakable words, which it is not lawful for a man to utter; and whether this had happened to him in the body or out of the body, he declares himself unable to say; but yet he has no fear of encountering from you comparison with the cattle. His spirit knew that it was in the third heaven, in paradise; but knew not whether it was in the body. The third heaven, of course, and paradise were not the Apostle Paul himself; but his body and soul and spirit were himself. Behold, then, the curious fact: he knew the great things—lofty and divine—which were not himself; but that which appertained to his own nature he was ignorant of. Who in the vast knowledge of such occult things can help being astonished at his great ignorance of his own existence? Who, in short, would believe it possible, if one who errs not had not told us, that "we know not what we should pray for as we ought"? Where, then, ought our bent and purpose mainly to be—to "reach forth to those things which are before"? And yet you compare me to cattle, if among the things which are behind I have forgotten anything concerning my own origin—although you hear the same apostle say: "Forgetting those things which are behind, and reaching forth unto those things which are before, I press toward the mark, for the prize of the high calling of God in Christ Jesus."

Chapter 13 [IX.]—In What Sense the Holy Ghost is Said to Make Intercession for Us.

Do you perhaps also think me ridiculous and like the irrational beasts, because I said, "We know not what we should pray for as we ought"? Perhaps this is not quite so intolerable. For since, in the dictates of a sound and righteous judgment, we prefer our future to our past; and since our prayer must have reference not to what we have been, but what we shall be, it is of course much more injurious not to know what we should pray for, than to be ignorant of the manner of our origin. But recollect whose words I repeated, or read them again for yourself, and reflect whence they come; and do not pelt me with your reproaches, lest the stone you throw should alight on a head you would not wish. For it is the great teacher of the Gentiles, the Apostle Paul himself, who said, "For we know not what we should pray for as we ought." And he not only taught this lesson by word, but also illustrated it by his example. For, contrary to his own advantage and the promotion of his own salvation, he once in his ignorance prayed that "the thorn in the flesh might depart from him," which he said had been given to him "lest he should be exalted above measure by the abundance of the revelations which were given him." But the Lord loved him, and so did not do what he had requested Him to do. Nevertheless, when the apostle said, "We know not what we should pray for as we ought," he immediately added, "But the Spirit Himself makes intercession for us with groanings which cannot be uttered. And He that searches the hearts knows what is the mind of the Spirit, because He makes intercession for the saints according to the will of God"—that is to say, He makes the saints offer intercessions. He, of course, is that Spirit "whom God hath sent into our hearts, crying, Abba, Father;" and "by whom we cry, Abba, Father;" for both expressions are used by the apostle—both that we have received the Spirit who cries, Abba, Father; and also that it is through Him that we cry, Abba, Father. His object is to explain by these varied statements in what sense he used the word "crying:" he meant causing to cry; so that it is we who cry at His instance and impulse. Let Him therefore teach me this too, whenever He pleases, if He knows it to be expedient for me, that I should know whence I derive my origin about my soul. But let me be taught by that Spirit who searches the deep things of God; not by a man who knows nothing of the breath which inflates a bag. However, be it far from me to compare you with brutes because of this piece of ignorance; because it arose not from incurable inability, but from sheer inadvertence.

Chapter 14 [X.]—It is More Excellent to Know That the Flesh Will Rise Again and Live for Evermore, Than to Learn Whatever Scientific Men Have Been Able to Teach Us Concerning Its Nature.

But although the questions which arise touching the origin of souls are "higher," no doubt, than that which treats of the source whence the breath comes which we inhale and exhale, you yet believe that those things are "higher" which you have learnt out of the Holy Scriptures, from which we derive what we learn by faith; and such as are not traceable by any human minds. Of course, it is far more excellent to know that the flesh will rise again and will live for evermore, than anything that scientific men have been able to discover in it by careful examination, which the soul perceives by no outward sense, although its presence quickens all the things of which it is ignorant. It is also far better to know that the soul, which has been born again and renewed in Christ, will be blessed forever, than to discover all that we are ignorant of touching its memory, understanding, and will. Now these subjects, which I have designated as more excellent and as better, we could by no means find out, unless we believed them on the testimony of the inspired Scriptures. These Scriptures you perhaps think you so thoroughly believe, that you do not hesitate to draw out of them a definite theory about the origin of souls. Well, then, first of all, if it be as you suppose, you ought never to have attributed to human nature itself what man knows by discussion and inquiry about his own nature and quality, but to God's gift. Now you asked: "Wherein does a man differ from the cattle, if he is ignorant of this?" But why need we read anything, in order to know this, if we ought already to know it by the very fact that we are different from cattle? For just as you do not read anything to me for the purpose of teaching me that I am alive (my own nature making it impossible that I should be ignorant of this fact), so if it is an attribute of nature to know this other matter, why do you produce passages of Scripture for me to believe concerning this subject? Is it then only those persons who read them that differ from the cattle? Are we not so created as to be different from brute animals, even before we can acquire the art of reading? Pray, tell me how it is that you put in so high a claim for our nature, that by the very circumstance of its differing from cattle it already knows how to discuss and inquire into the origin of souls; while at the same time you make it so inexpert in this knowledge, as to be unable by human endowment to know this without it believe the divine testimonies.

Chapter 15 [XI.]—We Must Not Be Wise Above What is Written.

But then, again, you are mistaken in this matter; for the passages of Scripture which you chose to produce for the solution of this question of yours, do not prove the point. For it is another thing which they prove, without which we cannot really lead a pious life, namely, that we have in God the giver, creator, and fashioner of our souls. But how He does this for them, whether by inbreathing them as new, or by deriving them from the parents, they do not tell us—except in the instance of that one soul which He gave to the first man. Read attentively what I have written to that servant of God, our brother Renatus; for since I have pointed it all out to him there, it is not necessary for me to repeat my proofs here. But you would like me to follow your example in definiteness of theory, and so thrust myself into such difficulties as you have surrounded yourself with. Involved in these, you have spoken many stout words against the catholic faith; if, however, you would faithfully and humbly bethink yourself and consider, you would assuredly see how greatly it would have profited you, if you had only known how to be natural and consistent in your ignorance; and how this advantage is still open to you, if you were even now able to maintain such propriety. Now, since understanding so pleases you in man's nature (for, truly enough, if our nature were without it, we should not be different from brute beasts, so far as our souls are concerned), understand, I beg of you, what it is that you do not understand, lest you should understand nothing: and do not despise any man who, in order that he may truly understand, understands that he does not understand that which he does not understand. With regard, however, to the passage in the inspired psalm, "Man, being in honor, understand not; he is compared to the senseless cattle, and is like unto them;" read and understand these words, that you may rather with a humble spirit guard against the opprobrium yourself, than arrogantly throw it out against another person. The passage applies to those who regard only that as a life worth living which they live in the flesh—having no hope after death—just like "cattle;" it has no reference to those who never deny their knowledge of what they actually know, and always acknowledge their ignorance of what they really do not know; who, in point of fact, are aware of their weakness, rather than confident of their strength.

Chapter 16. —Ignorance is Better Than Error. Predestination to Eternal Life, and Predestination to Eternal Death.

Do not, my son, let senile timidity displease your youthful confidence. For my own part, indeed, if I proved unequal, either under the teaching of God or of some spiritual instructor, to the task of understanding the subject of our present inquiry on the origin of souls, I am more prepared to vindicate God's righteous will, that we should remain in ignorance on this point, as on many others, than to say in my rashness what either is so obscure that I can neither bring it home to the intelligence of other people, nor understand it myself; or certainly even to help the cause of the heretics who endeavor to persuade us that the souls of infants are entirely free from guilt, on the ground, forsooth, that such guilt would only recoil on God as its Author, for having compelled innocent souls (for the help of which He knew beforehand no laver of regeneration was prepared) to become sinful, by assigning them to sinful flesh without any provision for that grace of baptism which should prevent their incurring eternal damnation. For the fact undoubtedly is, that numberless souls of infants pass out of the body before they are baptized. God forbid that I should cast about for any futile effort to dilute this stern fact, and say

A Treatise on the Soul and its Origin

what you have yourself said: "That the soul deserved to be polluted by the flesh, and to become sinful, though it previously had no sin, because of which it could be rightly said to have incurred this desert." And again: "That even without baptism original sins may be remitted." And once more: "That even the kingdom of heaven is at last bestowed on those who have not been baptized." Now, if I were not afraid to utter these and similar poisonous allegations against the faith, I should probably not be afraid to propound some definite theory on this subject. How much better, then, is it, that I should not separately dispute and affirm about the soul, what I am ignorant of; but simply hold what I see the apostle has most plainly taught us: That owing to one man all pass into condemnation who are born of Adam unless they are born again in Christ, even as He has appointed them to be regenerated, before they die in the body, whom He predestinated to everlasting life, as the most merciful bestower of grace; whilst to those whom He has predestinated to eternal death, He is also the most righteous awarder of punishment not only on account of the sins which they add in the indulgence of their own will, but also because of their original sin, even if, as in the case of infants, they add nothing thereto. Now this is my definite view on that question, so that the hidden things of God may keep their secret, without impairing my own faith.

Chapter 17 [XII.]—A Twofold Question to Be Treated Concerning the Soul; Is It "Body"? and is It "Spirit"? What Body is.

And now, as far as the Lord vouchsafes to enable

me, I must reply also to that allegation of yours, in which, speaking of the soul, you again mention my name, and say, "We do not, as the very able and learned bishop Augustin professes, allow it to be incorporeal and also a spirit." We have therefore, first, to discuss the question, whether the soul is to be deemed incorporeal, as I have said; or corporeal, as you hold. Then, secondly, whether in our Scriptures it is called a spirit—although not the whole but its own separate part is also properly called spirit. Well, I should, to begin with, like to know how you define body. For if that is not "body" which does not consist of limbs of flesh, then the earth cannot be a body, nor the sky, nor a stone, nor water, nor the stars, nor anything of the kind. If, however, a "body" is whatever consists of parts, whether greater or less, which occupy greater or smaller local spaces, then all the things which I have just mentioned are bodies; the air is a body; the visible light is a body; and so are all the things which the apostle has in view, when he says, "There are celestial bodies, and bodies terrestrial."

Chapter 18. —The First Question, Whether the Soul is Corporeal; Breath and Wind, Nothing Else Than Air in Motion.

Now whether the soul is such a substance, is an extremely nice and subtle question. You, indeed, with a promptitude for which I very greatly congratulate you, affirm that God is not a body. But then, again, you give me some anxiety when you say, "If the soul lacks body, so as to be (as some persons are pleased to suppose) of hollow emptiness, of airy and futile substance." Now, from these words you seem to believe, that everything which lacks body is of an empty substance. Well, if this is the case, how do you dare to say that God lacks body, without fearing the consequence that He is of an empty substance? If, however, God has not a body, as you have just allowed; and if it be profane to say that He is of an empty substance; then not everything which lacks body is an empty substance. And therefore, a person who contends that the soul is incorporeal does not necessarily mean, that it is of an empty and futile substance; for he allows that God, who is not an empty being, is at the same time incorporeal. But observe what great difference there is between my actual assertion, and what you suppose me to say. I do not say that the soul is an airy substance; if I did, I should admit that it is a body. For air is a body; as all who understand what they say declare, whenever they speak concerning bodily substances. But you, because I called the soul incorporeal, supposed me not only to predicate mere emptiness of it, but, as the result of such predication, to say that it is "an airy substance;" whereas I must have said both that it has not corporeity, which air has, and that what is filled with air could not be empty. And your own bag similes failed to remind you of this. For when the bags are inflated, what is it but air that is pressed into them? And they are so far from being empty, that because of their distension they become even ponderous. But perhaps the breath seems to you to be a different thing from air; although your very breath is nothing else than air in motion; and what this is, can be seen from the shaking of a fan. With respect to any hollow vessels, which you may supposed to be empty, you may ascertain with certainty that they are really full, by lowering them straight into the water, with the mouth downwards. You see no water can get in, because of the air with which they are filled. If, however, they are lowered either in the opposite way, with mouth upward, or aslant, they then fill, as the water enters at the same opening where the air passes out and escapes. This could be, of course, more easily proved by performing the experiment, than by a description in writing. This, however, is not the time or place for longer delay on the subject; for whatever may be your perception of the nature of the air, as to whether it has corporeity or not, you certainly ought not to suppose me to have said that the soul is an aerial thing, but absolutely incorporeal. And this even you acknowledge God to be, whom you do not dare to describe as an empty substance, while you cannot but admit that He has an essence which is unchangeable and almighty. Now, why should we fear that the soul is an empty void, if it be incorporeal, when we confess that God is incorporeal, and at the same time deny Him to be an empty void? Thus, it was within the competency of an Incorporeal Being to create an incorporeal soul, even as the living God made living man; although, as the unchangeable and the almighty, He communicated not these attributes to the changeable and far inferior creature.

Chapter 19 [XIII.]—Whether the Soul is a Spirit.

But again, why you would have the soul to be a body, and refuse to deem it a spirit, I cannot see. For if it is not a spirit, because the apostle named it with distinction from the spirit, when he said, "I pray God your whole spirit, and soul, and body be preserved," the same is a good reason why it is not a body, since he named the body, too, as distinct from it. If you affirm that the soul is a body, although they are both distinctly named; you should allow it to be a spirit, although these are also distinctly named. Indeed, the soul has a much greater claim to be regarded by you as a spirit than a body; because you acknowledge the spirit and the soul to be of one substance, but deny the soul and the body to be of one substance. On what principle, then, is the soul a body, when its nature is different from that of a body; and not a spirit, although its nature and a spirit's is one and the same? Why, according to your argument, must you not confess that even the spirit is a body? For otherwise, if the spirit is not a body, and the soul is a body, the soul and the spirit are not of one and the same substance. You, however, allow them both (although believing them to be two separate things) to have one substance. Therefore, if the soul is a body, the spirit is a body also; for under no other condition can they be regarded as being of one and the same nature. On your own principles, therefore, the statement of the apostle, who mentions, "Your spirit, and soul, and body," must imply three bodies; yet the body, which has likewise the name of flesh, is of a different nature. And of these three bodies, as you would call them, of which one is of a different, and the other two of one and the same substance, the entire human being is composed—one thing and one existence. Now, although you assert this, yet you will not allow that the two which are of one and the same substance, that is, the soul and the spirit, should have the one designation of spirit; whilst the two things which are not of one and the same substance ought, as you suppose, to have the one name of body.

Chapter 20 [XIV.]—The Body Does Not Receive God's Image.

But I pass by all this, lest the discussion between us should degenerate into one of names rather than things. Let us, then, see whether the inner man be the soul, or the spirit, or both. I observe, however, that you have expressed your opinion on the point in writing, calling the inner man the soul; for of this you spoke when you said: "And as the substance congealed, which was incapable of comprehension, it would produce another body within the body rounded and amassed by the force and twirl of its own nature, and thus an inner man would begin to appear, who, being molded in a corporeal sheath would in its lineaments be shaped after the likeness of its outer man." And from this you draw the following inference: "God's breath, therefore, made the soul; yea, that breath from God was made the soul, an image, substantial, corporeal according to its own nature, like its own body, and conformed to its image." After this you proceed to speak of the spirit, and say: "This soul which had its origin from the breath of God could not exist without an innermost sense and intellect of its own; and such is the spirit." As I, then, understand your statement, you mean the inner man to be the soul, and the inmost one to be the spirit; as if the latter were inferior to the soul, as this is to the body. Whence it comes to pass, that just as the body receives another body pervading its own inner cavity, which (as you suppose) is the soul; so in its turn must the soul be regarded as having its interior emptiness also, where it could receive the third body, even the spirit; and thus the whole man consists of three, the outer, the inner, and the inmost. Now, do you not yet perceive what great absurdities follow in your wake, when you attempt the asseveration that the soul is corporeal? Tell me, I pray you, which of the two is it that is to be renewed in the knowledge of God, after the image of Him that created him? The inner, or the inmost? For my own part, indeed, I do not see that the apostle, besides the inner and the outer man, knows anything of another man inside the inner one, that is, of an inmost man. But you must decide which it is you would have to be renewed after the image of God. How is he to receive this, who has already got the image of the outer man? For if the inner man has run throughout the limbs of the outward one, and congealed (for this is the term you have used; as if a molten shape were formed out of soft clay, which was thickened out of the dust), how, if this same figure which has been impressed upon it, or rather expressed out of a body, is to retain its place, could it be refashioned after the image of God? Is it to have two images—God's from above, that of the body from below—as is said in the case of money, "Heads and Tails"? Will you perhaps say, that the soul received the bodily image, and that the spirit takes God's image, as if the former were contiguous to the body, and the latter to God; and that, therefore, it is really the inmost man which is refashioned after the image of God, and not the inner man? Well, but this presence is useless. For if the inmost man is as entirely diffused through all the members of the soul, as the inner man of the soul is through the limbs of the body; even it has now, through the soul, received the image of the body, as the soul molded the same; and thus it results that it has no means whereby to receive God's image, while the afore-mentioned image of the body remains impressed upon it; except as in the case of the money which I have just quoted, where there is one form on the upper surface, and another on the lower one. These are the absurd lengths to which you are driven, whether you will or no, when you apply to the consideration of the soul the material ideas of bodily substances. But, as even you yourself with perfect propriety confess, God is not a body. How, then, could a body receive His image? "I beseech you, brother, that you be not conformed to this world, but be transformed by the renewing of your mind;" and cherish not "the carnal mind, which is death."

Chapter 21 [XV.]—Recognition and Form Belong to Souls as Well as Bodies.

But you say: "If the soul is incorporeal, what was it that the rich man saw in hell? He certainly recognized Lazarus; he did [not] know Abraham. Whence arose to him the knowledge of Abraham, who had died so long before?" By using these words, I suppose that you do not think a man can be recognized and known without his bodily form. To know yourself, therefore, I imagine that you often stand before your looking-glass, lest by forgetting your features you should be unable to recognize yourself. But let me ask you, what man does anybody know more than himself; and whose face can he see less than his own? But who could possibly know God, whom even you do not doubt to be incorporeal, if knowledge could not (as you suppose) accrue without bodily shape; that is, if bodies alone can be recognized? What Christian, however, when discussing subjects of such magnitude and difficulty, can give such little heed to the inspired word as to say, "If the soul be incorporeal, it must of necessity lack form"? Have you forgotten that in that word you have read of "a form of doctrine"? Have you forgotten, too, that it is written concerning Christ Jesus, before His clothing Himself with humanity, that He was "in the form of God"? How, then, can you say, "If the soul is incorporeal, it must of necessity lack form;" when you hear of "the form of God," whom you acknowledge to be incorporeal; and so express yourself, as if form could not possibly exist except in bodies?

Chapter 22. —Names Do Not Imply Corporeity.

You also say, that "names cease to be given, when form is not distinguished; and that, where there is no designation of persons, there is no giving of names." Your aim is to prove that Abraham's soul was corporeal, since he could be addressed as "Father Abraham." Now, we have already said, that there is form even where there is no body. If, however, you think that where there are not bodies there is no assigning of names, I must beg of you to count the names which occur in this passage of Scripture, "But the fruit of the Spirit is love, joy, peace, long-suffering, gentleness, goodness, faith, meekness, temperance," and tell me whether you do not recognize the very things of which these are the names; or whether you recognize them so as to descry some outlines of bodies. Come, tell me, to mention only love, for instance, what are its members, its figure, its color? For if you are not yourself empty-headed, these appurtenances cannot possibly be regarded by you as an empty thing. Then you go on to say: "The look and form must, of course, be corporeal of him whose help is implored." Well, let men hear what you say; and let no one implore God's help, because no one can possibly see anything corporeal in Him.

Chapter 23 [XVI.]—Figurative Speech Must Not Be Taken Literally.

"In short," you say, "members are in this parable ascribed to the soul, as if it were really a body." You will have it, that "by the eye the whole head is understood," because it is said, that "he lifted up his eyes." Again you say, that "by tongues are meant jaws, and by finger the hand," because it is said, "Send Lazarus, that he may dip the tip of his finger in water, and cool my tongue." And yet to save yourself from the inconsistency of ascribing corporeal qualities to God, you say that "by these terms must be understood incorporeal functions and powers;" because with the greatest propriety you insist on it, that God is not corporeal. What is the reason, therefore, that the names of these limbs do not argue corporeity in God, although they do in the case of the soul? Is it that these terms must be understood literally when spoken of the creature, and only metaphorically and figuratively when predicated of the Creator? Then you will have to give us wings of literal bodily substance, since it is not the Creator, but only a human creature, who said, "If I should take my wings like a dove." Moreover, if the rich man of the parable had a bodily tongue, on the ground of his exclaiming, "Let him cool my tongue," it would look very much as if our tongue, even while we are in the flesh, itself possessed material hands, because it is written, "Death and life are in the hands of the tongue." I suppose it is even to yourself self-evident, that sin is neither a creature nor a bodily substance; why, then, has it a face? For do you not hear the psalmist say, "There is no peace in my bones, in the face of my sins"?

Chapter 24. —Abraham's Bosom—What It Means.

As to your supposing that "the Abraham's bosom referred to is corporeal," and your further assertion, that "by it is meant his whole body," I fear that you must be regarded (even in such a subject) as trying to joke and raise a laugh, instead of acting gravely and seriously. For you could not else be so foolish as to think that the material bosom of one person could receive so many souls; nay, to use your own words, "bear the bodies of as many meritorious men as the angels carry thither, as they did Lazarus." Unless it happens to be your opinion, that his soul alone deserved to find its way to the said bosom. If you are not, then, in fun, and do not wish to make childish mistakes, you must understand by "Abraham's bosom" that remote and separate abode of rest and peace in which Abraham now is; and that what was said to Abraham did not merely refer to him personally, but had reference to his appointment as the father of many nations, to whom he was presented for imitation as the first and principal example of faith; even as God willed Himself to be called "the God of Abraham, the God of Isaac, and the God of Jacob," although He is the God of an innumerable company.

Chapter 25 [XVII.]—The Disembodied Soul May Think of Itself Under a Bodily Form.

You must not, however, suppose that I say all this as if denying it to be possible that the soul of a dead man, like a person asleep, may think either good or evil thoughts in the similitude of his body. For, in dreams, when we suffer anything harsh and troublesome, we are, of course, still ourselves; and if the distress do not pass away when we awake, we experience very great suffering. But to suppose that they are veritable bodies in which we are hurried, or flit, about hither and thither in dreams, is the idea of a person who has thought only carelessly on such subjects; for it is in fact mainly by these imaginary sights that the soul is proved to be non-corporeal; unless you choose to call even the objects which we see so often in our dreams, besides ourselves, bodies, such as the sky, the earth, the sea, the sun, the moon, the stars, and rivers, mountains, trees, or animals. Whoever takes these phantoms to be bodies, is incredibly foolish; although they are certainly very like bodies. Of this character also are those phenomena which are demonstrably of divine significance, whether seen in dreams or in a trance. Who can possibly trace out or describe their origin, or the material of which they consist? It is, beyond question, spiritual, not corporeal. Now things of this kind, which look like bodies, but are not really corporeal, are formed in the thoughts of persons when they are awake, and are held in the depths of their memories, and then out of these secret recesses, by some wonderful and ineffable process, they come out to view in the operation of our memory, and present themselves as if palpably before our eyes. If, therefore, the soul were a material body, it could not possibly contain so many things and such large forms of bodily substances in its scope of thought, and in the spaces of its memory; for, according to your own definition, "it does not exceed this external body in its own corporeal substance." Possessing, therefore, no magnitude of its own, what capacity has it to hold the images of vast bodies, spaces, and regions? What wonder is it, then, if it actually itself appears to itself in the likeness of its own body, even when it appears without a body? For it never appears to itself in dreams with its own body; and yet in the very similitude of its own body it runs hither and thither through known and unknown places, and beholds many sad and joyous sights. I suppose, however, that you really would not, yourself, be so bold as to maintain that there is true corporeity in that form of limb and body which the soul seems to itself to possess in dreams. For at that rate that will be a real mountain which it appears to ascend; and that a material house which it seems to enter; and that a veritable tree, with real wood and bulk, beneath which it apparently reclines; and that actual water which it imagines itself to drink. All the things with which it is conversant, as if they were corporeal, would be undoubted bodies, if the soul were itself corporeal, as it ranges about amongst them all in the likeness of a body.

Chapter 26 [XVIII.]—St. Perpetua Seemed to Herself, in Some Dreams, to Have Been Turned into a Man, and Then Have Wrestled with a Certain Egyptian.

Some notice must be taken of sundry accounts of martyrs' visions, because you have thought proper to derive some of your evidence therefrom. St. Perpetua, for instance, seemed to herself in dreams to be wrestling with an Egyptian, after being changed into a man. Now, who can doubt that it was her soul in that apparent bodily form, not her body, which, of course, remained in her own sex as a woman, and lay on the bed with her senses steeped in sleep, whilst her soul was struggling in the similitude of a man's body? What have you to say to this?

Was that male likeness a veritable body, or was it no body at all, although possessing the appearance of a body? Choose your alternative. If it was a body, why did it not maintain its sexual integrity? For in that woman's flesh were found no virile functions of generation, whence by any such process as that which you call congelation could be molded this similitude of a man's body. We will conclude then, if you please, that, as her body was still alive while she slept, notwithstanding the wrestling of her soul, she remained in her own natural sex, enclosed, of course, in all her proper limbs which belong to her in her living state, and was still in possession of that bodily shape and the lineaments of which she had been originally formed. She had not resigned, as she would by death, her joints and limbs; nor had she withdrawn from the transposing power, which arises from the operation of the power of death, any of her members which had already received their fixed form. Whence, then, did her soul get that virile body in which she seemed to wrestle with her adversary? If, however, this [male likeness] was not a body, although such a semblance of one as admitted the sensation in it of a real struggle or a real joy, do you not by this time see, as far as may be, that there can be in the soul a certain resemblance of a bodily substance, while the soul is not itself a body?

Chapter 27. —Is the Soul Wounded When the Body is Wounded?

What, then, if some such thing is exhibited among the departed; and souls recognize themselves among them, not, indeed, by bodies, but by the semblances of bodies? Now, when we suffer pain, if only in our dreams, although it is only the similitude of bodily limbs which is in action, and not the bodily limbs themselves, still the pain is not merely in semblance, but in reality; as is also the case in the instance of joyous sensations. Inasmuch, however, as St. Perpetua was not yet dead, you probably are unwilling to lay down a precise rule for yourself from that circumstance (although it bears strongly on the question), as to what nature you will suppose those semblances of bodies to partake of, which we have in our dreams. If you allow them to be like bodies, but not bodies actually, then the entire question would be settled. But her brother Dinocrates was dead; she saw him with the wound which he received while alive, and which caused his death. Where is the ground for the earnest contention to which you devoted your efforts, when you labored to show, that when a limb is cut off, the soul must not be supposed as suffering a like amount of loss by amputation? Observe, the wound was inflicted on the soul of Dinocrates, expelling it by its force from his body, when it was inhabiting that body. How, then, can your opinion be correct, that "when the limbs of the body are cut off, the soul withdraws itself from the stroke, and after condensation retires to other parts, so that no portion of it is amputated with the wound inflicted on the body," even if the person be asleep and unconscious when the loss of limb is suffered? So great is the vigilance which you have ascribed to the soul, that even should the stroke fall on any part of the flesh without its knowledge, when it is absorbed in the visions of dreams, it would instantly, and by a providential instinct, withdraw itself, and so render it impossible for any blow, or injury, or mutilation to be inflicted upon it. However, you may, as much as you will, ransack your ingenuity for an answer to the natural question, how the soul withdraws the portions of its own existence, and retreats within itself, so that, whenever a limb of the body is cut off or broken, it does not suffer any amputation or fracture in itself; but I cannot help asking you to look at the case of Dinocrates, and to explain to me why his soul did not withdraw from that part of his body which received the mortal wound, and so escape from suffering in itself what was plainly enough seen in his face, even after his body was dead? Is it, perchance, your good pleasure that we should suppose the phenomena in question to be rather the semblances of bodies than the reality; so that as that which is really no wound seems to be a wound, so that which is no body at all wears the appearance of corporeity? If, indeed, the soul can be wounded by those who wound the body, should we not have good reason to fear that it can be killed also by those who kill the body? This, however, is a fate which the Lord Himself most plainly declares it to be impossible to happen. And the soul of Dinocrates could not at any rate have died of the blow which killed his body: its wound, too, was only an apparent one; for not being corporeal, it was not really wounded, as the body had been; possessing the likeness of the body, it shared also the resemblance of its wound. Still it may be further said, that in its unreal body the soul felt a real misery, which was signified by the shadow of the body's wound. It was from this real misery that he earned deliverance by the prayers of his holy sister.

Chapter 28. —Is the Soul Deformed by the Body's Imperfections?

Now, again, what means it that you say, "The soul

acquires form from the body, and grows and extends with the increase of the body," without keeping in view what a monstrosity the soul of either a young man or an old man would become if his arm had been amputated when he was an infant? "The hand of the soul," you say, "contracts itself, so that it is not amputated with the hand of the body, and by condensation it shrinks into other parts of the body." At this rate the aforesaid arm of the soul will be kept, wherever it holds its ground, as short as it was at first when it received the form of the body, because it has lost the form by the growth of which it might itself have increased at an equal degree of expansion. Thus, the soul of the young man or the old man who lost his hand in his infancy advances with two hands, indeed (because the one which shrank back escaped the amputation of the bodily limb), but one of these was the hand of an adult, young or old, according to the hypothesis, while the other was only an infant's hand, just as it was when the amputation happened. Such souls, believe me, are not made in the mold and form of the body, but they are fictitiously framed under the deformed stamp of error. It seems to me impossible for you to be rescued from this error, unless with God's help you fully and calmly examine the visions of those who dream, and from these convince yourself that some forms are not real bodies, but only the semblances of bodies. Now, although even those objects which we supposed to be like bodies are of the same class, yet so far as the dead are concerned, we can form an after guess about them from persons who are asleep. For it is not in vain that Holy Scripture describes as "asleep" those who are dead were it only because in a certain sense "sleep is akin to death."

Chapter 29 [XIX.]—Does the Soul Take the Body's Clothes Also Away with It?

If, indeed, the soul were body, and the form were also a corporeal figure in which it sees itself in dreams, because it received its expression from the body in which it is enclosed: not a human being, if he lost a limb, would in dreams see himself bereft of the amputated member, although actually deprived of it. On the contrary, he would always appear to himself entire and unmutilated, from the circumstance that no part has been cut away from the soul itself. But since persons sometimes see themselves whole and sometimes mutilated in limb, when this happens to be their actual plight, what else does this fact show than that the soul, both in respect of other things seen by it in dreams and about the body, bears about, hither and thither, not their reality, but only their resemblance? The soul's joy, however, or sadness, its pleasure or pain, are severally real emotions, whether experienced in actual or in apparent bodies. Have you not yourself said (and with perfect truth): "Aliments and vestments are not wanted by the soul, but only by the body"? Why, then, did the rich man in hell crave for the drop of water? Why did holy Samuel appear after his death (as you have yourself noticed) clothed in his usual garments? Did the one wish to repair the ruins of the soul, as of the flesh, by the aliment of water? Did the other quit life with his clothes on him? Now in the former case there was a real suffering, which tormented the soul; but not a real body, such as required food. While the latter might have seemed to be clothed, not as being a veritable body, but a soul only, having the semblance of a body with a dress. For although the soul extends and contracts itself to suit the members of the body, it does not similarly adapt itself to the clothes, so as to fit its form to them.

Chapter 30. —Is Corporeity Necessary for Recognition?

But who can trace out what capacity of recognition even souls which are not good possess after death when relieved of the corruptible bodies, so as to be able by an inner sense to observe and recognize either souls that are evil like themselves, or even good ones, either in states which are actually not corporeal, but the semblances of bodies; or else in good or evil affections of the mind, in which there occur no lineaments whatever of bodily members? Whence arises the fact that the rich man in the parable, though in torments, recognized "Father Abraham," whose face and figure he had never seen, but the semblance of whose body his soul, though incorporeal, was able to comprehend? But who could rightly say that he had known any man, except in so far as he has had means of knowing his life and disposition, which have, of course, neither material substance nor colors? It is in this way that we know ourselves more certainly than any others, because our own consciousness and disposition are all before us. This we plainly perceive, and yet we see therein no similitude of a bodily substance. But we do not perceive this inner quality of our nature in another man, even if he be present before our eyes; though in his absence we recollect his features, and recognize them, and think of them. Our own features, however, we cannot in the same manner recollect, and recognize, and think of; and yet with most perfect truth we say that we are ourselves better known to ourselves than he is, so manifest is it where lies the stronger and truer knowledge of man.

Chapter 31 [XX.]—Modes of Knowledge in the Soul Distinguished.

Forasmuch, then, as there is one function in the soul, by which we perceive real bodies, which we do by the five bodily senses; another, which enables us to discern apart from these non-corporeal likenesses of bodies (and by this we can have a view of ourselves also, as not otherwise than like to bodies); and a third, by which we gain a still surer and stronger insight into objects fitted for its faculty, which are neither corporeal nor are like bodily substances,—such as faith, hope, charity,—things which have neither complexion, nor passion, nor any such thing: on which of these functions ought we to dwell more intently, and to some degree more familiarly, and where be renewed in the knowledge of God after the image of Him who created us? Is it not on and in that which I have now put in the third place? And here we shall certainly experience neither sexual difference nor the semblance thereof.

Chapter 32. —Inconsistency of Giving the Soul All the Parts of Sex and Yet No Sex.

For that form of the soul, whether masculine or feminine, which has the distinction of members characteristic of man and woman, being no semblance merely of body, but actual body, is either a male or a female, whether you will or no, precisely as it appears to be a man or a woman. But if your opinion be correct, and the soul is a body, even a living body, then it both possesses swelling and pendent breasts, and lacks a beard, it has a womb, and all the generative organs of a woman, yet is not a woman after all. Will not mine, then, be a statement more consistent with truth: the soul, indeed, has an eye and has a tongue, has a finger, and all other members which resemble those of the body, and yet the whole is the semblance of a body, not a body really? My statement is open to a general test; everybody can prove it in himself, when he brings home to his mind the image of absent friends; he can prove it with certainty when he recalls the figures both of himself and other persons, which have occurred to him in his dreams. On your part, however, no example can throughout nature be produced of such a monstrosity as you have imagined, where there is a woman's real and living body, but not a woman's sex.

Chapter 33. —The Phoenix After Death Coming to Life Again.

Now, what you say about the phoenix has nothing whatever to do with the subject before us. For the phoenix symbolizes the resurrection of the body; it does not do away with the sex of souls; if indeed, as is thought, he is born afresh after his death. I suppose, however, that you thought your discourse would not be sufficiently plausible unless you declaimed a good deal about the phoenix, after the fashion of young people. Now do you find in the body of your bird male organs of generation and not a male bird; or female ones, and not a female? But, I beg of you, reflect on what it is you say, —what theory you are trying to construct, and to recommend for our acceptance. You say that the soul, spread through all the limbs of the body, grew stiff by congelation, and received the entire shape of the whole body from the crown of the head to the soles of the feet, and from the inmost marrow to the skin's outward surface. At this rate it must have received, in the case of a female body, all the inner appurtenances of a woman's body, and yet not be a woman! Why, pray, are all the members feminine in a true living body, and yet the whole no woman? And why all be male, and the result not a man? Who can be so presumptuous as to believe, and profess, and teach all this? Is it that souls never generate? Then, of course, mules and she-mules are not male and female. Is it that souls without bodies of flesh would be unable to cohabit? Well, but this deprivation is shared by castrated men; and yet, although both the process and the motion be taken from them, their sex is not removed—some slender remnant of their male members being still left to them. Nobody ever said that a eunuch is not a male. What now becomes of your opinion, that the souls even of eunuchs have the generative organs unimpaired, and that these organs will remain entire, on your principle, in their souls, even when they are clean removed from their bodily structure? For you say, the soul knows how to withdraw itself when that part of the flesh begins to be cut off, so that the form which has been removed when amputated is not lost; but although spread over it by condensation, it retires by an extremely rapid movement, and so buries itself within as to be kept quite safe; yet that cannot, forsooth, be a male in the other world which carries with it thither the whole appendage of male organs of generation, and which, if it had not even other signs in the body, was a male by reason of those organs alone. These opinions, my son, have no truth in them; if you will not allow that there is sex in the soul, there cannot be a body either.

Chapter 34 [XXI.]—Prophetic Visions.

Not every semblance of a body is itself a body. Fall asleep and you will see this; but when you awake again, carefully discern what it is you have seen. For in your dreams you will appear to yourself as if endued with a body; but it really is not your body, but your soul; nor is it a real body, but the semblance of a body. Your body will be lying on the bed, but the soul walking; the tongue of your body will be silent, but that of your soul in the dream will talk; your eyes will be shut, but your soul will be awake; and, of course, the limbs of your body stretched out in your bed will be alive, not dead. Consequently that congealed form, as you regard it, of your soul is not yet extracted, as it were, out of its sheath; and yet in it is seen the whole and perfect semblance of your fleshly frame. Belonging to this class of similitudes of corporeity, which are not real bodies, though they seem to be such, are all those appearances which you read of in the Holy Scriptures in the visions even of the prophets, without, however, understanding them; by which are also signified the things which come to pass in all time—present, past, and future. You make mistakes about these, not because they are in themselves deceptive, but because you do not accept them as they ought to be taken. For in the same apocalyptic vision where "the souls of the martyrs" are seen, there is also beheld "a lamb as it were slain, having seven horns:" there are also horses and other animals figuratively described with all consistency; and lastly, there were the stars falling, and the earth rolled up like a book; nor does the world, despite all, then actually collapse. If therefore we understand all these things wisely, although we say they are true apparitions, yet we do not call them real bodies.

Chapter 35. —Do Angels Appear to Men in Real Bodies?

It would, however, require too lengthy a discourse to enter very carefully on a discussion concerning this kind of corporeal semblances; whether angels even, either good ones or evil ones, appear in this manner, whenever they appear in the likeness of human beings or of any bodies whatever; or whether they possess real bodies, and show themselves in this veritable state of corporeity; or, again, whether by persons when dreaming, indeed, or in a trance they are perceived in these forms—not in bodies, but in the likeness of bodies—while to persons when awake they present real bodies which can be seen, and, if necessary, actually touched. Such questions as these, however, I do not deem it at all requisite to investigate and fully treat in this book. By this time enough has been advanced respecting the soul's incorporeity. If you would rather persist in your opinion that it is corporeal, you must first of all define what "body" means; lest, peradventure, it may turn out that we are agreed about the thing itself, but laboring to no purpose about its name. The absurd conclusions, however, to which you would be reduced if you thought of such a body in the soul, as are those substances which are called "bodies" by all learned men, —I mean such as occupy portions of space, smaller ones for their smaller parts, and larger ones for their larger, — by means of the different relations of length and breadth and thickness, I venture to think you are by this time able intelligently to observe.

Chapter 36 [XXII.]—He Passes on to the Second Question About the Soul, Whether It is Called Spirit.

It now remains for me to show how it is that while the designation spirit is rightly predicated of a part of the soul, not the whole of it,—even as the apostle says, "Your whole spirit, and soul, and body;" or, according to the much more expressive statement in the Book of Job, "Thou wilt separate my soul from my spirit,"—yet the whole soul is also called by this name; although this question seems to be much more a question of names than of things. For since it is certainly a fact that there is a something in the soul which is properly called "spirit," while (this being left out of question) it is also designated with equal propriety "soul," our present contention is not about the things themselves; mainly because I on my side certainly admit, and you on your part say the same, that that is properly called spirit by which we reason and understand, and yet that these things are distinguishingly designated, as the apostle says "your whole spirit, and soul, and body." This spirit, however, the same apostle appears also to describe as mind; as when he says, "So then with the mind I serve the law of God, but with the flesh the law of sin." Now the meaning of this is precisely what he expresses in another passage thus: "For the flesh lusted against the spirit, and the spirit against the flesh." What he designates mind in the former place, he must be understood to call spirit in the latter passage. Not as you interpret the statement, "The whole mind is meant, which consists of soul and spirit,"—a view which I know not where you obtained. By our "mind," indeed, we usually understand nothing but our rational and intellectual faculty; and thus, when the apostle says, "Be ye renewed in the spirit of your mind," what else does he mean than, Be ye renewed in your mind? "The spirit of the mind" is, accordingly, nothing else than the mind, just as "the body of the flesh" is nothing but the flesh; thus it is written, "In putting off the body of the flesh," where the apostle calls the flesh "the body of the flesh." He designates it, indeed, in another point of view as the spirit of man, which he quite distinguishes from the mind: "If," says he, "I pray with the tongue, my spirit prays, but my mind is unfruitful." We are not now, however, speaking of that spirit which is distinct from the mind; and this involves a question relating to itself which is really a difficult one. For in many ways and in divers senses the Holy Scriptures make mention of the spirit; but with respect to that we are now speaking of, by which we exercise reason, intelligence, and wisdom, we are both agreed that it is called (and indeed rightly called) "spirit," in such a sense as not to include the entire soul, but a part of it. If, however, you contend that the soul is not the spirit, because the understanding is distinctly called "spirit," you may as well deny that the whole seed of Jacob is called Israel, since, apart from Judah, the same appellation was distinctly and separately borne by the ten tribes which were then organized in Samaria. But why need we linger any longer here on this subject?

Chapter 37 [XXIII.]—Wide and Narrow Sense of the Word "Spirit."

But now, with a view to our easier elucidation, I beg you to observe that what is the soul is also designated spirit in the scripture which narrates an incident in our Lord's death, thus, "He bowed His head and gave up the spirit." Now, when you hear or read these words, you wish to understand them as if the whole were signified by a part, and not because that which is the soul may also be called spirit. But I shall, for the purpose of being able the more readily to prove what I say, actually summon yourself with all promptitude and convenience as my witness. For you have defined spirit in such terms that cattle appear not to have a spirit, but a soul. Irrational animals are so called, because they have not the power of intelligence and reason. Accordingly, when you admonished man himself to know his own nature, you spoke as follows: "Now, since the good God has made nothing without a purpose, He has produced man himself as a rational animal, capable of intelligence, endowed with reason, and enlivened by sensibility, so as to be able to distribute in a wise arrangement all things that are void of reason." In these words of yours you have plainly asserted what is certainly most true, that man is endowed with reason and capable of intelligence, which, of course, animals void of reason are not. And you have, in accordance with this view, quoted a passage of Scripture, and, adopting its language, have compared men of no understanding to the cattle, which, of course, have not intellect. A statement the like to which occurs in another passage of Scripture: "Be ye not as the horse or as the mule, which have no understanding." This being the case, I want you also to observe in what terms you have defined and described the spirit when trying to distinguish it from the soul: "This soul," you say, "which has its origin from the breath of God, could not have possibly been without an inner sense and intellect of its own; and this is the spirit." A little afterwards you add: "And although the soul animates the body, yet since it possesses sense, and wisdom, and vigor, there must needs be a spirit." And then somewhat further on you say: "The soul is one thing, and the spirit—which is the soul's wisdom and sense—is another." In these words, you plainly enough indicate what you take the spirit of man to mean; that it is even our rational faculty, whereby the soul exercises sense and intelligence, —not, indeed, the sensation which is felt by the bodily senses, but the operation of that innermost sense from which arises the term sentiment. Owing to this it is, no doubt, that we are placed above brute animals, since these are unendowed with reason. These animals therefore have not spirit, —that is to say, intellect and a sense of reason and wisdom, —but only soul. For it is of these that it was spoken, "Let the waters bring forth the creeping creatures that have a living soul;" and again, "Let the earth bring forth the living soul." In order, indeed, that you may have the fullest and clearest assurance that what is the soul is in the usage of the Holy Scriptures also called spirit, the soul of a brute animal has the designation of spirit. And of course, cattle have not that spirit which you, my beloved brother, have defined as being distinct from the soul. It is therefore quite evident that the soul of a brute animal could be rightly called "spirit" in a general sense of the term; as we read in the Book of Ecclesiastes, "Who knows the spirit of the sons of men, whether it goes upward; and the spirit of the beast, whether it goes downward into the earth?" In like manner, touching the devastation of the deluge, the Scripture testifies, "All flesh died that moved upon the earth, both of fowl, and of cattle, and of beast, and of every creeping thing that creeps upon the earth, and every man: and all things which have the spirit of life." Here, if we remove all the windings of doubtful disputation, we understand the term spirit to be synonymous with soul in its general sense. Of so wide a signification is this term, that even God is called "a spirit;" and a stormy blast of the air, although it has material substance, is called by the psalmist the "spirit" of a tempest. For all these reasons, therefore, you will no longer deny that what is the soul is called also spirit; I have, I think, adduced enough from the pages of Holy Scripture to secure your assent in passages where the soul of the very brute beast, which has no understanding, is designated spirit. If, then, you take and wisely consider what has been advanced in our discussion about the incorporeity of the soul, there is no further reason why you should take offence at my having said that I was sure the soul was not body, but spirit, —both because it is proved to be not corporeal, and because in its general sense it is denominated spirit.

Chapter 38 [XXIV.]—Victor's Chief Errors Again Pointed Out.

Wherefore if you take these books, which I have with a sincere and affectionate interest written in answer to your opinions, and read them with a reciprocal love for me; if you attend to what you have yourself declared in the beginning of your first book, and "are anxious not to insist on any opinion of your own, if it be found an improbable one," then I beseech you to beware especially of those eleven errors which I warned you of in the preceding book of this treatise. Do not say, that "the soul is of God in such a sense that He created it not out of no, nor out of another, but out of His own nature;" or that, "as

God who gives is Himself ever existent, so is He ever giving souls through infinite time;" or that "the soul lost some merit through the flesh, which it had previous to the flesh;" or that "the soul by means of the flesh repairs its ancient condition, and is born again through the very same flesh, by which it had deserved to be polluted;" or that "the soul deserved to be sinful even prior to sin;" or that "infants who die without the regeneration of baptism, may yet attain to forgiveness of their original sins;" or that "they whom the Lord has predestinated to be baptized can be taken away from His predestination, or die before that has been accomplished in them which the Almighty had predetermined;" or that "it is of those who expire before they are baptized that the Scripture says, 'Speedily was he taken away, lest wickedness should alter his understanding,'"—with the remainder of the passage to the same effect; or that "there are some mansions outside the kingdom of God, belonging to the 'many,' which the Lord said were in His Father's house;" or that "the sacrifice of the body and blood of Christ ought to be offered in behalf of those who have departed out of the body without being baptized;" or that "any of those persons who die without Christ's baptism, are received for a while into paradise, and afterwards attain even to the blessedness of the kingdom of heaven." Above all things, beware of these opinions, my son, and, as you wish to be the vanquisher of error, do not rejoice in the surname of "Vincentius." And when you are ignorant on any subject, do not think that you know it; but in order to get real knowledge, learn how to be ignorant. For we commit a sin by affecting to be ignorant of nothing among "the secret things of God;" by constructing random theories about unknown things, and taking them for known; and by producing and defending errors as if they were truth. As for my own ignorance on the question whether the souls of men are created afresh at every birth, or are transmitted by the parents (an ignorance which is, however, modified by my belief, which it would be impious to falter in, that they are certainly made by the Divine Creator, though not of His own substance), I think that your loving self-will by this time be persuaded that it either ought not to be censured at all, or, if it ought, that it should be done by a man who is capable by his learning of removing it altogether; and so also with respect to my other opinions, that while souls have in them the incorporeal semblances of bodies, they are not themselves bodies; and that, without impairing the natural distinction between soul and spirit, the soul is in a general sense actually designated spirit. If, indeed, I have unfortunately failed to persuade you, I must leave it rather to my readers to determine whether what I have advanced ought not to have convinced you.

Chapter 39. —Concluding Admonition.

If, as may possibly be the case, you desire to know whether there are many other points which appear to me to require emendation in your books, it cannot be troublesome for you to come to me, —not, indeed, as a scholar to his master, but as a person in his prime to one full of years, and as a strong man to a weak one. And although you ought not to have published your books, still there is a greater and a truer glory in a man's being censured, when he confesses with his own lips the justice of his correction, than in being lauded out of the mouth of any defender of error. Now, while I should be unwilling to believe that all those who listened to your reading of the afore-mentioned books, and lavished their praises on you, had either previously held for themselves the opinions which sound doctrine disapproves of, or were induced by you to entertain them, I still cannot help thinking that they had the keenness of their mind blunted by the impetuous and constant flow of your elocution, and so were unable to bestow adequate attention on the contents of your discourse; or else, that when they were in any case capable of understanding what you said, it was less for any very clear statement of the truth that they praised you than for the affluence of your language, and the facility and resources of your mental powers. For praise, and fame, and kindly regard are very commonly bestowed on a young man's eloquence in anticipation of the future, though as yet it lacks the mellowed perfection and fidelity of a fully-informed instructor. In order, then, that you may attain to true wisdom yourself, and that what you say may be able not only to delight, but even edify other people, it behooves you, after removing from your mind the dangerous applause of others, to keep conscientious watch over your own words.

www.ingramcontent.com/pod-product-compliance
Lightning Source LLC
Chambersburg PA
CBHW052032070526
44584CB00016B/2010